A World of
Poetry
for CXC

Edited by:
Mark McWatt and
Hazel Simmons-McDonald

www.caribbeanschools.co.uk

Heinemann
Inspiring generations

Heinemann Educational Publishers
Halley Court, Jordan Hill, Oxford OX2 8EJ
Part of Harcourt Education

Heinemann is a registered trademark of
Harcourt Education Limited

© Harcourt Education, 2005
CXC logo © Caribbean Examinations Council

First published 2005

10 09 08 07 06 05
10 9 8 7 6 5 4 3

British Library Cataloguing in Publication Data is available
from the British Library on request

ISBN-10: 0 435 98801 8
ISBN-13: 987 0435 98801 2

Designed and typeset by Tek-Art, Croydon

Original illustrations © Harcourt Education Limited, 2005

Illustrated by Phyllis Mahon

Cover design by Wooden Ark Studio

Printed by Biddles Ltd

Cover illustrations by Petrina Wright

Contents

CONTENTS

PEOPLE AND DESIRES

FROM TIME TO ETERNITY

The following icon is used in this book:

p.000 This indicates the page number of the notes and questions which accompany the poem or vice versa.

Introduction

Dear students and teachers,

In this revised edition of the 1994 anthology, we have removed 49 of the original 138 poems and replaced them with 49 new ones. We have tried to replace each poem with one of a similar theme that offers an appropriately comparable challenge to the reader. The new poems roughly maintain the balance between poems from earlier periods and those of contemporary poets.

While we have organised the book into twelve sections reflecting the dominant themes of the poems, we do not intend this organisation to dictate the order in which you read them. You will discover that several of the poems explore more than one theme and may fit just as well into a different section. Teachers, you may wish to choose two (or more) poems from any of the thematic groups and devise questions that will help your students to read the poems carefully while focusing their attention on the broader themes.

As you are probably aware, CXC specifically tests a candidate's ability to compare and synthesise information from two or more sources. To develop this skill, you can devise questions on two poems having the same theme or even on individual poems, particularly the longer ones, that will focus on the way(s) in which their different parts relate to each other and to the central idea or theme.

You may find the notes and questions at the end of each section useful for initiating discussion on individual poems. Our questions are not exhaustive, and they do not focus on every aspect of the poems deserving comment. Students, we think it is important for you to interpret, analyse and explore the deeper levels of meaning in the poems, and that too long a list of questions might restrict your discussions and limit the process of discovery.

We have also included general information on poetic genre and form, and notes on figurative language. We hope that these will help you to recognise poetic devices when you encounter them in your reading, and that you will be better able to understand why they are used and how they contribute to the overall richness and meaning of individual poems. The sample questions and answers at the back of the book will give you an idea of the difference between a good and a weak answer, and of the way(s) in which you should approach questions in the CXC examination.

While we have chosen several poems that we think a CXC candidate should study, we have also tried to include poems that will appeal to your interests. We hope that you will experience delight and intellectual stimulation from reading the poems in this book.

Mark McWatt and Hazel Simmons-McDonald

The Child and the World

This picture illustrates the poem, 'Childhood', on page 32 in this section.

Nature

Childhood of a Voice

The light oppresses and the darkness frees
a man like me, who never cared at all:
Imagine it, the childhood of a voice
and voice of childhood telling me my name.

5   But if only the rain would fall,
and the sky we have not seen so long
come blue again.

The familiar white street
is tired of always running east.
10 The sky, of always arching over.
The tree, of always reaching up.

Even the round earth is tired of being round
and spinning round the sun.

Martin Carter

Sea Wall

(Excerpt from *Belize Suite*)

Only a gentle swish
Where waves would touch the land
no wind no turbulence
along this wall arranged by man
5 dividing land from sea

No cruise-ships light this harbour end to end
only that cluster
where the army lights
ride there at anchor . . .
10 cool darkness and deluding calm

houses sit silent near the water's edge
their calm precarious like our peace
hoisted on stilts
like mokojumbies in the carnival
15 listening the ocean's gentle murmur
hearing its angry wail
what seems like decades now
when death rode loud and furious
on the hissing waves

20 From storm and earthquake Lord
deliver us
and us
and us

p.15 *Velma Pollard*

A Lesson for this Sunday

The growing idleness of summer grass
With its frail kites of furious butterflies
Requests the lemonade of simple praise
In scansion gentler than my hammock swings
5 And rituals no more upsetting than a
Black maid shaking linen as she sings
The plain notes of some protestant hosanna
Since I lie idling from the thought in things,

Or so they should. Until I hear the cries
10 Of two small children hunting yellow wings,
Who break my sabbath with the thought of sin.
Brother and sister, with a common pin,
Frowning like serious lepidopterists.
The little surgeon pierces the thin eyes.
15 Crouched on plump haunches, as a mantis prays
She shrieks to eviscerate its abdomen.
The lesson is the same. The maid removes
Both prodigies from their interest in science.
The girl, in lemon frock, begins to scream
20 As the maimed, teetering thing attempts its flight.

She is herself a thing of summery light.
Frail as a flower in this blue August air,
Not marked for some late grief that cannot speak.

The mind swings inward on itself in fear
25   Swayed towards nausea from each normal sign.
Heredity of cruelty everywhere,
And everywhere the frocks of summer torn,
The long look back to see where choice is born,
As summer grass sways to the scythe's design.

p.15 *Derek Walcott*

The Sound of Trees

I wonder about the trees.
Why do we wish to bear
Forever the noise of these
More than another noise
5   So close to our dwelling place?
We suffer them by the day
Till we lose all measure of pace,
And fixity in our joys,
And acquire a listening air.
10   They are that that talks of going
But never gets away;
And that talks no less for knowing,
As it grows wiser and older,
That now it means to stay.
15   My feet tug at the floor
And my head sways to my shoulder
Sometimes when I watch trees sway,
From the window or the door.
I shall set forth for somewhere,
20   I shall make the reckless choice
Some day when they are in voice
And tossing so as to scare
The white clouds over them on.
I shall have less to say,
25   But I shall be gone.

p.16 **Robert Frost**

The Moor

It was like a church to me.
I entered in on soft foot,
Breath held like a cap in the hand.
It was quiet.
5   What God was there made himself felt,
Not listened to, in clean colours
That brought a moistening of the eye,
In movement of the wind over grass.

There were no prayers said. But stillness
10   Of the heart's passions – that was praise
Enough; and the mind's cession
Of its kingdom. I walked on,
Simple and poor, while the air crumbled
And broke on me generously as bread.

p.16   *R. S. Thomas*

Pheasant

You said you would kill it this morning.
Do not kill it. It startles me still,
The jut of that odd, dark head, pacing

Through the uncut grass on the elm's hill.
5   It is something to own a pheasant,
Or just to be visited at all.

I am not mystical: it isn't
As if I thought it had a spirit.
It is simply in its element.

10   That gives it a kingliness, a right.
The print of its big foot last winter,
The tail-track, on the snow in our court –

The wonder of it, in that pallor,
Through crosshatch of sparrow and starling.
15   Is it its rareness, then? It is rare.

But a dozen would be worth having,
A hundred, on that hill – green and red,
Crossing and recrossing: a fine thing!

It is such a good shape, so vivid.
20   It's a little cornucopia.
It unclaps, brown as a leaf, and loud,

Settles in the elm, and is easy.
It was sunning in the narcissi.
I trespass stupidly. Let be, let be.

p.16   *Sylvia Plath*

Birdshooting Season

Birdshooting season the men
make marriages with their guns
My father's house turns macho
as from far the hunters gather

5   All night long contentless women
stir their brews: hot coffee
chocolata, cerassie
wrap pone and tie-leaf
for tomorrow's sport. Tonight
10   the men drink white rum neat.

In darkness shouldering
their packs, their guns, they leave

We stand quietly on the
doorstep shivering. Little boys
15   longing to grow up birdhunters too
Little girls whispering:
Fly Birds Fly.

p.16   *Olive Senior*

Schooldays

Every nun wears a ring
– Brides of God.
An astonishing act,
as if depictions of hell
5   came true with brush-marks
and artists cheering.

Rain is wetting windows,
but what about trees
witnessing the Bride of God
10   deprive little boys of sin.

For each nun, God and boy,
strings of colour
and separate balconies
link all realities as
15   another astonishing act.
But the sunset is yours,
the garden of guavas mine,
and God can have the rest.

p.17   **Stanley Greaves**

The Prize Cat

Pure blood domestic, guaranteed,
Soft-mannered, musical in purr,
The ribbon had declared the breed,
Gentility was in the fur.

5   Such feline culture in the gads,
No anger ever arched her back –
What distance since those velvet pads
Departed from the leopard's track!

And when I mused how Time had thinned
10   The jungle strains within the cells,
How human hands had disciplined
Those prowling optic parallels;

I saw the generations pass
Along the reflex of a spring,
15 A bird had rustled in the grass,
The tab had caught it on the wing:

Behind the leap so furtive-wild
Was such ignition in the gleam,
I thought an Abyssinian child
20 Had cried out in the whitethroat's scream.

p.17 *E. J. Pratt*

Rain Storm

This rage of waterangels
On zinc
Occurs when clouds touch
River.

5 The rotten gutter spews
Disintegrating jets
Of silver water
Crystal spinning droplets

Into the
10 Murky river
Bares her frothy
Underwear at thunder touch.

There is God and
You
15 In every drop
And droplet
Every liquid touch
And touchlet
Every streak of lightning
20 And every slap of thunder

Sees you and God
And I
Melt into each other.

p.17 **Sasenarine Persaud**

An African Thunderstorm

From the west
Clouds come hurrying with the wind
Turning
Sharply
5 Here and there
Like a plague of locusts
Whirling
Tossing up things on its tail
Like a madman chasing nothing.
10 Pregnant clouds
Ride stately on its back
Gathering to perch on hills
Like dark sinister wings;
The Wind whistles by
15 And trees bend to let it pass.

In the village
Screams of delighted children
Toss and turn
In the din of the whirling wind.
20 Women –
Babies clinging on their backs –
Dart about
In and out
Madly
25 The Wind whirls by
Whilst trees bend to let it pass.
Clothes wave like tattered flags
Flying off
To expose dangling breasts
30 As jaggered blinding flashes
Rumble, tremble, and crack
Amidst the smell of fired smoke
And the pelting march of the storm.

p.17 *David Rubadiri*

9

Those Winter Sundays

Sundays too my father got up early
and put his clothes on in the blueblack cold,
then with cracked hands that ached
from labor in the weekday weather made
5   banked fires blaze. No one ever thanked him.

I'd wake and hear the cold splintering, breaking.
When the rooms were warm, he'd call,
and slowly I would rise and dress,
fearing the chronic angers of that house,

10   Speaking indifferently to him,
who had driven out the cold
and polished my good shoes as well.
What did I know, what did I know
of love's austere and lonely offices?

p.18   *Robert Hayden*

A Contemplation Upon Flowers

Brave flowers, that I could gallant it like you,
And be as little vain;
You come abroad and make a harmless show,
And to your beds of earth again;
5   You are not proud, you know your birth,
For your embroidered garments are from earth.

You do obey your months and times, but I
Would have it ever spring;
My fate would know no winter, never die,
10   Nor think of such a thing;
Oh that I could my bed of earth but view,
And smile and look as cheerfully as you.

Oh teach me to see death and not to fear,
But rather to take truce;
15   How often have I seen you at a bier,
And there look fresh and spruce;
You fragrant flowers then teach me that my breath
Like yours may sweeten and perfume my death.

p.18   *Henry King*

Janet Waking

Beautifully Janet slept
Till it was deeply morning. She woke then
And thought about her dainty-feathered hen,
To see how it had kept.

5   One kiss she gave her mother.
One a small one gave she to her daddy
Who would have kissed each curl of his shining baby
No kiss at all for her brother.

'Old Chucky, old Chucky!' she cried.
10   Running across the world upon the grass
To Chucky's house, and listening. But alas,
Her Chucky had died.

It was a transmogrifying bee
Came droning down on Chucky's old bald head
15   And sat and put the poison. It scarcely bled,
But how exceedingly

And purply did the knot
Swell with the venom and communicate
Its rigor! Now the poor comb stood up straight
20   But Chucky did not.

So there was Janet
Kneeling on the wet grass, crying her brown hen
(Translated far beyond the daughters of men)
To rise and walk upon it.

25   And weeping fast as she had breath
Janet implored us, 'Wake her from her sleep!'
And would not be instructed in how deep
Was the forgetful kingdom of death.

p.18 *John Crowe Ransome*

Traveling Through the Dark

Traveling through the dark I found a deer
dead on the edge of the Wilson River road.
It is usually best to roll them into the canyon:
that road is narrow; to swerve might make more dead.

5   By glow of the tail-light I stumbled back of the car
and stood by the heap, a doe, a recent killing;
she had stiffened already, almost cold.
I dragged her off; she was large in the belly.

My fingers touching her side brought me the reason –
10   her side was warm; her fawn lay there waiting,
alive, still, never to be born.
Beside that mountain road I hesitated.

The car aimed ahead its lowered parking lights;
under the hood purred the steady engine.
15   I stood in the glare of the warm exhaust turning red;
around our group I could hear the wilderness listen.

I thought hard for us all – my own swerving –,
then pushed her over the edge into the river.

p.18 *William Stafford*

A Comfort of Crows

Mark this for a mercy: that here
birds, even here, sustain
the wide and impossible highways
of warm currents, divide the sky;
5   mark this – they all day have
amazed the air, that it falls apart
from their heavy wings in thin wedges
of sound; though the dull black earth
is very still, sweating
10   a special sourness
they make high over the hard thorn-trees
their own magnificence, turning,
they chain all together
with very slow journeys to and fro
15   the limits of the dead place,
smelling anything old and no longer quick.

Even here, though the rough ground
offers no kindness to the eye
nor the rusting engines could not ever
20   have intended an excellence of motion
and the stones have fallen in strange attitudes
and the boxes full of dry stained paper –
above the harsh barrows of land and metal
great birds pursue a vigilant silence.
25   The ceremonies of their soaring
have made a new and difficult solace:
there is no dead place nor dying so terrible
but weaves above it surely, breaking
the fragile air with beauty of its coming,
30   a comfort as of crows . . .

p.19   *Dennis Scott*

Responsibility

I half awaken
to the comforting blur of my mother
pulling on her house-
dress in the half dark

5 and already the sound of my father
as from muted dream distance
clucking the chickens to corn.

I too some distant morning
shall rise responsibly
10 to set my house in motion.

Meantime, I pull the covers close
and smile for the pure secret
thrill of it, and ease myself down
into that last, sweet, morning sleep.

p.19 *Edward Baugh*

Notes and questions

Some of the poems in this section describe the simple beauty of nature while others focus on wild life and the hunting of animals. Other selections are about pets and some explore the effect of the loss of pets on their owners. The power of the elements and death as an inevitable natural occurrence are other themes reflected here.

p.2 *Childhood of a Voice*

- What is the persona of this poem longing for?
- How would you describe the mood of the speaker of the poem?
- How do the last six lines of the poem (lines 8–13) emphasise this mood?
- Discuss the title of the poem with your classmates. How appropriate is it for the subject matter that the poem deals with?

p.2 *Sea Wall*

'mokojumbies' (line 14) – term used to refer to costumed stilt-dancers in Trinidad carnival.

- What exactly is the poet contrasting, and why does she present the extended description in stanzas 1 and 2?
- What is the point the poet makes in stanza 3? Do you think it justifies the prayerful ending of the poem? Why or why not?

p.3 *A Lesson for this Sunday*

'lepidopterists' (line 13) – people who study and/or collect moths/butterflies.
'heredity' (line 26) – transmission of genetic factors (that determine individual characteristics) from one generation to another.

- What is the poet doing in the first stanza and what is he musing about?
- What were the children doing in stanza 2 that disturbed the poet?
- What is the point of the poet's statement about the girl in the last three lines of stanza 2?
- What do you think 'Heredity of cruelty everywhere' (line 26) means in the context of the last stanza and the rest of the poem? Explain the lesson referred to in the title of the poem.

The Sound of Trees

- What is the attitude expressed towards the sound of trees in lines 1–9?
- Who are the 'they' and what is the 'that' referred to in line 9?
- Explain the image in and meaning of lines 15 and 16.
- What do you think is the 'reckless choice' (line 19) that the persona will make?
- Taking your answer to the previous question into consideration, discuss the meaning of the last 11 lines (15–25) of the poem.

The Moor

Title: moor – an expanse of waste ground usually covered with wild plants and scrub like bracken, moss, heather and coarse grass.

- The poet compares his visit to the moor with a visit to a church. Find the things that are most like what goes on in a church and the things that are different.
- What is the effect of this visit on the persona of the poem?

Pheasant

Title: pheasant – a long-tailed bird; the males have brightly coloured plumage.
'cornucopia' (line 20) – literally 'the horn of plenty', a horn-shaped container usually filled with fruit and other food, symbolising the earth's abundance.
'narcissi' (line 23) – a plant with yellow, orange or white flowers which have a crown surrounded by spreading segments.

- The poet does not want the pheasant to be killed. Find all the reasons she gives for sparing it.
- In lines 3–12 the poet describes the pheasant in detail. Why? What can you tell about her own response to the pheasant from these lines?
- To whom, do you think, are the words, 'Let be, let be' (line 24) addressed?

Birdshooting Season

- Explain what is meant by 'the men/make marriages with their guns' (lines 1–2).
- Why are the women described as 'contentless'?
- Explain the difference in the attitudes between the males and females towards the hunting season.

Schooldays

p.7

- What is the 'astonishing act' referred to in line 3 of the poem?
- The persona expresses scepticism in the first stanza. What is he sceptical about?
- What do you think is the 'sin' referred to in line 10?
- In your own words explain what exactly the trees witness.
- The images in the last stanza are presented as in a painting. Pick out these images and explain what the 'astonishing act' (line 15) is.
- What point is the poet stressing in the assertions made in the last three lines of the poem?

The Prize Cat

p.7

'The ribbon' (line 3) – the strip of cloth indicating an award or prize.
'in the gads' (line 5) – literally sharp spikes of metal. Here it refers to the retractable claws of the cat.
'Abyssinian child' (line 19) – child from Abyssinia or Ethiopia.
'whitethroat' (line 20) – a kind of European warbler usually brown with a whitish throat and belly.

- In stanzas 1, 2 and 3 the poet describes the way in which the cat has become domesticated. Find words or phrases that highlight the domestic qualities and fine breeding of the cat.
- What point about the cat is the poet making in 'Departed from the leopard's track!' (line 8)?
- To what does the phrase 'optic parallels' (line 12) refer?
- What happens in the last two stanzas that constitutes a contrast to the description in the first three stanzas?

Rain Storm

p.8

- The poet describes a rainstorm and reflects on what it means; at what point in the poem does description end and reflection begin?
- What qualities of the storm does the poet focus on in the description?
- What point is the poet making in the last three lines of the poem?

An African Thunderstorm

p.9

- The poet uses several different images to describe the gathering storm. Focus on these images and discuss the specific effects the poet creates with each one.

- What is the effect of the repetition of 'The wind . . . pass' at the end of stanza 1 (lines 14–15) and stanza 2 (lines 25–26)?
- Look carefully at the diction (choice of words and phrases). What is particularly striking about it?

p.10 *Those Winter Sundays*

'indifferently' (line 10) – showing no care, concern or interest.

- Consider the things that the father does. What do they suggest about him?
- What was the son's attitude towards the father when he was a child? How has it changed?
- What do you think are the 'chronic angers' of the house (line 9)?
- Explain the last two lines of the poem.

p.10 *A Contemplation Upon Flowers*

- What is the lifecycle of flowers as presented in the poem?
- What are the things about the flowers that the poet would like to emulate?

p.11 *Janet Waking*

'transmogrify' (line 13) – to change or transform into a different shape, especially a bizarre or grotesque one.

- What point is being emphasised, do you think, by the description of Janet's way of greeting her family (stanza 2) and her response to the hen (stanzas 3, 6 and 7)?
- Explain what happened to the hen.
- Discuss with your classmates the appropriateness and significance of the title of the poem.

p.12 *Traveling Through the Dark*

Focus on the following points as part of your discussion of this poem.

- Why does the poet hesitate?
- What does '– my only swerving' (line 17) suggest about the poet's intention in this instance?
- How do you view the poet's action (line 18) in the context of lines 12–18?

p.13 ## A Comfort of Crows

- What is the significance of the title of this poem?
- The poet uses the phrase 'even here' in line 2 of the poem and repeats it in line 17. Discuss the reasons for and the effect of the repetition.

p.14 ## Responsibility

- What, in the view of the persona of the poem, are the things that represent responsibility?
- With what are these things contrasted?
- Consider the use of the following phrases 'comforting blur', 'muted dream distance' and comment on their contribution to the meaning of the poem.

Childhood Experiences

Colonial Girls School

For Marlene Smith MacLeish

Borrowed images
willed our skins pale
muffled our laughter
lowered our voices
5 let out our hems
dekinked our hair
denied our sex in gym tunics and bloomers
harnessed our voices to madrigals
and genteel airs
10 yoked our minds to declensions in Latin
and the language of Shakespeare

    Told us nothing about ourselves
    There was nothing about us at all

How those pale northern eyes and
15 aristocratic whispers once erased us
How our loudness, our laughter
debased us

    There was nothing left of ourselves
    Nothing about us at all

20 Studying: *History Ancient and Modern*
Kings and Queens of England
Steppes of Russia
Wheatfields of Canada

    There was nothing of our landscape there
25   Nothing about us at all

Marcus Garvey turned twice in his grave.
'Thirty-eight was a beacon. A flame.
They were talking of desegregation

in Little Rock, Arkansas, Lumumba
30 and the Congo. To us mumbo-jumbo.
We had read Vachel Lindsay's
vision of the jungle

   Feeling nothing about ourselves
   There was nothing about us at all

35 Months, years, a childhood memorising
Latin declensions
(For our language
– 'bad talking' –
detentions)

40   Finding nothing about us there
       Nothing about us at all

So, friend of my childhood years
One day we'll talk about
How the mirror broke
45 Who kissed us awake
Who let Anansi from his bag

For isn't it strange how
northern eyes
in the brighter world before us now

50 Pale?

p.37   *Olive Senior*

Examination Centre

Dilapidated room,
paint peeling.
Sufferers
on edge.

5 The chief invigilator
gives the word.
The fingered papers rustle.

Outside the centre –
part of my recall –
10 trees bend and stretch
and breathe.
Winds, playful, tease.

We're struggling here
with questions
15 and time
and longing
for a life we glimpse
through dust
clouding the panes.

p.37 *Mervyn Morris*

Mid-Term Break

I sat all morning in the college sick bay
Counting bells knelling classes to a close.
At two o'clock our neighbours drove me home.

In the porch I met my father crying –
5 He had always taken funerals in his stride –
And Big Jim Evans saying it was a hard blow.

The baby cooed and laughed and rocked the pram
When I came in, and I was embarrassed
By old men standing up to shake my hand

10 And tell me they were 'sorry for my trouble',
Whispers informed strangers I was the eldest,
Away at school, as my mother held my hand

In hers and coughed out angry tearless sighs.
At ten o'clock the ambulance arrived
15 With the corpse, stanched and bandaged by the nurses.

Next morning I went up into the room. Snowdrops
And candles soothed the bedside; I saw him
For the first time in six weeks. Paler now,

Wearing a poppy bruise on his left temple,
20 He lay in the four foot box as in his cot.
No gaudy scars, the bumper knocked him clear.

A four foot box, a foot for every year.

p.38 *Seamus Heaney*

My Parents

My parents kept me from children who were rough
Who threw words like stones and who wore torn clothes.
Their thighs showed through rags. They ran in the street
And climbed cliffs and stripped by the country streams.

5 I feared more than tigers their muscles like iron
Their jerking hands and their knees tight on my arms.
I feared the salt coarse pointing of those boys
Who copied my lisp behind me on the road.

10 They were lithe, they sprang our behind hedges
Like dogs to bark at my world. They threw mud
While I looked the other way, pretending to smile.
I longed to forgive them, but they never smiled.

p.38 *Stephen Spender*

Journal

(For Melanie)

My daughter, bent
like a sapling
in the wind of her imagination
has cast off on an ocean
5 where I flounder
with each page
that washes by.

When she was born
I learned the swimmer's truth:
10 you drown if you can dream
of drowning, if you learn
to read too well.
I turned to treading water
then, narrowing
15 my eyes against
the salt of metaphor,
the dazzle of the sunlight
on the seas' bright margins.

I feared the white roar
20 underneath the silence
of the sun-struck afternoons.

Time, like an ocean, makes us
islands all. The sea-gulls
shriek across the arid green
25 of waves eroding every coast,
each half-moon of a beach
that limits every village
to an alphabet
of necessary gesture.

30 I built her paper boats
when she was three
out of discarded poems
and the letters I could never send to my father.

Now I wake up to lavender,
35 the sky above the blue ridge
bruised with light, the grey chill
edged with woodsmoke. Sometimes
she voyages all night, chained
to the mast of some unwieldy narrative.
40 I free her into sleep
at fore-day morning, then
I trudge down to the waiting water,
Hoping to drown again.

p.38   *David Williams*

24

A Song in the Front Yard

I've stayed in the front yard all my life.
I want to peek at the back
Where it's rough and untended and hungry weed grows.
A girl gets sick of a rose.

5   I want to go in the back yard now
And maybe down the alley,
To where the charity children play.
I want a good time today.

They do some wonderful things.
10   They have some wonderful fun.
My mother sneers, but I say it's fine
How they don't have to go in at quarter to nine.
My mother, she tells me that Johnnie Mae
Will grow up to be a bad woman.
15   That George'll be taken to Jail soon or late
(On account of last winter he sold our back gate).

But I say it's fine. Honest, I do.
And I'd like to be a bad woman, too,
And wear the brave stockings of night-black lace
20   And strut down the streets with paint on my face.

p.38   *Gwendolyn Brooks*

Ana

While she was yet too young to crawl
my pride would picture her sunlit, outside
playing with flowers
like every poet's child;
5   the frills of her pink dress
waving in the gentlest whim
of her father, observing,
pen in hand, her little gestures
in her world of green.

10 It was a calm and quiet mental scene.

Instead, now,
she leaps at me
off kitchen counters
when my arms and mind are full
15 of other things:
I glimpse the little hands
lunging for my throat,
and in that stiffening split-second
I wish she would miss
20 (serve her damn right)
I pray she won't miss
(little monkey)
but infallibly, I feel her hard fingers
her sharp nails
25 in the neutral father-flesh of my neck
and her barbaric howl of delight
stifles my angry shout.
I make to unhorse her with a wild shrug
she thinks it's a game,
30 'Do that again, Daddy',
and like a fool
Daddy does it again.

I've given up the prospect
of pink dresses and flowers;
35 I let her kick her somersaults

off my stomach, hardly noticing now
the muddy footprints on my shirts,
the scratches on my arms . . .
I think I must endure her thorny assaults
40 precisely because they seem
like self-inflicted wounds.

And yet when she is curled in sleep,
like a comma,
I can ponder still the possibility
45 of finishing all the stanzas
with images of her calm beauty
– lying so peaceful on the flower-patterned sheet,
all her brutal fangs of life
retracted behind the closed lids.

p.39 *Mark McWatt*

My Papa's Waltz

The whiskey on your breath
Could make a small boy dizzy;
But I hung on like death:
Such waltzing was not easy.

5 We romped until the pans
Slid from the kitchen shelf;
My mother's countenance
Could not unfrown itself.

The hand that held my wrist
10 Was battered on one knuckle;
At every step you missed
My right ear scraped a buckle.

You beat time on my head
With a palm caked hard by dirt,
15 Then waltzed me off to bed
Still clinging to your shirt.

p.39 *Theodore Roethke*

Counter

He was in prison,
his brother called to say.
I learned he was considered counter

to the ideas of the revolution,
5   that he planned with a counter group.
He was in prison.

I used to be his teacher, I explained.
He's young, I said, foolish perhaps, not dangerous.
I learned he was considered counter.

10   I saw his calm face in the second row
And knew I was too close to that distress.
He was in prison.

Months later, he was released, no charge.
I saw his listening face in the second row.
15   I learned he was considered counter.
Artist, teacher, vacillator, I found no counter answer.

p.39   *Merle Collins*

Little Boy Crying

Your mouth contorting in brief spite and hurt,
your laughter metamorphosed into howls,
your frame so recently relaxed now tight
with three-year-old frustration, your bright eyes
5   swimming tears, splashing your bare feet,
you stand there angling for a moment's hint
of guilt or sorrow for the quick slap struck.

The ogre towers above you, that grim giant,
empty of feeling, a colossal cruel,
10   soon victim of the tale's conclusion, dead
at last. You hate him, you imagine
chopping clean the tree he's scrambling down
or plotting deeper pits to trap him in.

You cannot understand, not yet,
15   the hurt your easy tears can scald him with,
nor guess the wavering hidden behind that mask.
This fierce man longs to lift you, curb your sadness
with piggy-back or bull-fight, anything,
but dare not ruin the lessons you should learn.

20   You must not make a plaything of the rain.

p.39   *Mervyn Morris*

Coming Out

A frightened mare
galloping down cobbled
streets on a stormy night;
your heartbeat fills the room.

5   Through the open window of the labour ward
the incinerator's smokestack looms.
But we're beyond such omens now,

all our attention focussed
on your *coming out*
10   in that pale blue frock of skin
with its bloody sequins;
our reluctant debutante.

Your mother, floating on 'Inspired Therapy',
launches you into your life's long ball.
15   You're a sensation! WOW!

And for me, no doubts,
it's love at first sight.
Your card's marked; I'm proud
to be your escort for the early dances.

p.39   *Stewart Brown*

Early Innocence

Remorse never came near it
when we sank puppies and kittens .
or when we whacked worms
to see how pieces wriggled.

5   It could have been called pure
how we tested birds-egg thinness
with knocks, and how we took
half full bags of fledglings
from summer woods.

10   Doubt came nowhere near
laughter ringing round us,
when we showed the sun
the weakling's willy, and made
the spastic boy eat dirt.

15   Nothing like trouble was about
when we caught and raced
the neighbour's pony, over
and over sultry pastureland
and swore with tears
20   the beast bathed in the pond.

But then early fun had not become
an expert's guide to living
to make the mute and the weak pay,
in jungle or city.

25   Every fish we hooked we cooked.
Every bird we shot was seasoned.

p.40   *James Berry*

Gull

My son brought home a seagull
with a damaged wing
his mother and sister helped
him fuss over it and feed the wild,
5   ungrateful thing.

They treated the raw, unfeathered
patch and tied the drooping limb
to its body with a strip of cloth;
deciding not to name him yet,
10   they placed him for the night
in a shoebox lined with an old towel
complete with plastic tot of water
and two smelly sprats, procured
with difficulty at such short warning.
15   The boy guessed all would be right,
come morning.

In fact the thing died.
When I checked before breakfast, it
was stiff, and its rank death
20   had already attracted a phalanx
of tiny ants. My son said nothing;
looked at it a while, then
dealt it an almighty kick, box and all
and sent it crashing into the opposite wall.

25   So much for the nameless bird.
Sister and mother were aghast,
upset he could be so uncaring,
But I understood why he kicked it,
and approved, beneath the mandatory frown.
30   I think it's right to kick at death,
especially when you're young.
He was not uncaring, what he cared for
was life, the chance to see the creature mend,
to release it and watch it soar;
35   the lifeless form was cruel recompense
for all the love and care he'd felt before

– and so he wanted no business
with dead things, his savage kick
focussed his argument more sharply
40 than these words, and I hope for him
a life as fiercely free as he had wanted
for that awkward, damaged bird.

p.40   *Mark McWatt*

Childhood

Rivers flow red and swollen with the clay
of upstream mountains where the
rains fall. Mockingbirds call
in the woods from the roseapple tree
5   echo the cry of crazy-lost children
and the bird-filled hills fear still
sudden death. By slingshot.

The dead in a certain graveyard
cannot rest again after a long ago
10 awakening when Sunday School children
hunted cashew nuts on the way to church
and wept over penny-for-the-collection-plate
lost in the cracks of the tombs.

At the river Job's Tears wait still
15 eager hands seeking treasure
for stringing and logwood blossom boats
float far as Falmouth – or China – bringing
a fleet of magical ships to all
lingering downstream. The day
20 could turn magic. From the river
tables rise and rivermaids comb
their hair golden in the afternoon
singing.

p.40   *Olive Senior*

Once Upon a Time

Once upon a time, son,
they used to laugh with their hearts
and laugh with their eyes;
but now they only laugh with their teeth,
5   while their ice-block-cold eyes
search behind my shadow.

There was a time indeed
they used to shake hands with their hearts;
but that's gone, son.
10   Now they shake hands without hearts
while their left hands search
my empty pockets.

'Feel at home'! 'Come again';
they say, and when I come
15   again and feel
at home, once, twice,
there will be no thrice –
for then I find doors shut on me.

So I have learned many things, son.
20   I have learned to wear many faces
like dresses – homeface,
officeface, streetface, hostface,
cocktailface, with all their conforming smiles
like a fixed portrait smile.

25   And I have learned, too,
to laugh with only my teeth
and shake hands without my heart.
I have also learned to say, 'Goodbye',
when I mean 'Good-riddance';
30   to say 'Glad to meet you',
without being glad; and to say 'It's been
nice talking to you', after being bored.

But believe me, son.
I want to be what I used to be

35   when I was like you. I want
      to unlearn all these muting things.
      Most of all, I want to relearn
      how to laugh, for my laugh in the mirror
      shows only my teeth like a snake's bare fangs!

40   So show me, son,
      how to laugh; show me how
      I used to laugh and smile
      once upon a time when I was like you.

p.41   *Gabriel Okara*

River Girl

For Linda T.

Throwing stones into the river
I caught a sudden leap of indirection
a splintering of the moon
that broke my own spectacle of reflection.
5   The shards of transparency shuffled
and there she stood, my river-maid.

Sudden as a waterfall
she stood before me:
I named her Carmen,
10   the first frantic song of my blood
roostering my sleep of indifference . . .
She shook her hair
and the stars shifted like flecks of river foam
and when she pinned my constellation
15   to her bosom, I thought
I would take her home.

River girls never come home
(I know that now)
so we danced instead
20   on that shore of origins

where showers of coloured rice-grains
fell like flowers at our feet
into the soiled river-wrack.
It was the moon that fashioned every moment's pose
25   and every flake of light upon her lips.

She left me then
with mere memory,
and yet how strong its stare
into the heart of that moment,
30   that visitation in my thirteenth year.
Even when the stars dimmed
and the river's fragments mended their vision,
I knew those ripples were not beyond recall;
were as intimate as my fingers
35   ready for all the rites.

p.41   *Mark McWatt*

Forgive My Guilt

Not always sure what things called sins may be,
I am sure of one sin I have done.
It was years ago, and I was a boy,
I lay in the frost flowers with a gun,
5   The air ran blue as the flowers; I held my breath,
Two birds on golden legs slim as dream things
Ran like quicksilver on the golden sand,
My gun went off, they ran with broken wings
Into the sea, I ran to fetch them in,
10   But they swam with their heads high out to sea,
They cried like two sorrowful high flutes,
With jagged ivory bones where wings should be.
For days I heard them when I walked that headland
Crying out to their kind in the blue,
15   The other plovers were going over south
On silver wings leaving these broken two.
The cries went out one day; but I still hear them
Over all the sounds of sorrow in war or peace
I ever have heard, time cannot drown them,

20   Those slender flutes of sorrow never cease.
     Two airy things forever denied the air!
     I never knew how their lives at last were split,
     But I have hoped for years all that is wild,
     Airy, and beautiful will forgive my guilt.

p.41   *Robert P. Tristram Coffin*

Notes and questions

The poems in this section reveal that there are experiences which are common to childhood regardless of the culture in which one may grow up. Several of the poems explore responses to experiences like taking examinations and participating in childish escapades. Others focus on more serious themes like death, cruelty and confusion. Most of the poems are narrated from an adult perspective and are reflective in nature. Think about your own experiences and discuss your own responses to the kinds of events and situations represented in the selection.

p.20 *Colonial Girls School*

Marcus Garvey (line 26) – leader of the 'Back-to-Africa' movement which started in Jamaica in 1914 and spread to the United States in 1916 when Garvey emigrated there. Garvey was born in 1887 and he died in Jamaica in 1940.

'Thirty-eight' (line 27) – the year 1938.

- Would you say that the experiences described in lines 1–11 are viewed as positive or negative?

- What, in the persona's view, are the shortcomings of the education she received?

- Are you familiar with the expression 'turn in one's grave'? What does it mean? Why does the poet say that Marcus Garvey 'turned twice in his grave' (line 26)?

- What is suggested by 'kissed us awake' (line 45)? Can you explain the allusion?

- What is the nature of the new awareness that the persona experiences?

- What is the effect of the repetition of 'nothing about us at all'?

p.21 *Examination Centre*

- The subject matter of this poem is undoubtedly very familiar to you. Recall examinations you have taken recently. Do you share similar feelings with the persona of the poem? Try writing a verse or two expressing your own responses to taking examinations.

37

p.22 | ## *Mid-Term Break*

- How does the word 'knelling' in stanza 1 prepare the reader for the events described in the poem?
- Who has died? Are any clues given in the poem as to the cause of death? If there are, what are the lines that indicate this?
- How does the persona respond to the event compared with the other people in the poem?

p.23 | ## *My Parents*

- There are implied differences between the persona of the poem and other children (line 1). What are those differences?
- What can you infer about the attitude of the persona towards the children?

p.23 | ## *Journal*

- The persona claims to be floundering in the 'ocean' cast off by his daughter. Do you think that this 'ocean' refers to the care and concerns of fatherhood or to the ocean of paper he was trying to write about her? Or both?
- Discuss with your fellow students the extended metaphor of swimming and drowning. What is the persona saying about his relationship with his daughter?
- Is this poem really about the persona's daughter, or about the persona himself?

p.25 | ## *A Song in the Front Yard*

- The poet is comparing two ways of life; one way is represented by the front yard and the other by the back yard. What are the differences between these two ways of life?
- What are the things about the back yard that the persona of the poem finds attractive?
- Discuss the image of the yard. How does it contribute to the meaning of the poem?
- Consider the title of the poem and discuss its appropriateness to the theme.
- The rhythm and rhyme scheme of the last stanza is different from that used in the other stanzas. Discuss the effectiveness of this stanza in relation to the first three stanzas and to the title and theme of the poem.

p.26 · *Ana*

- How does the poet's image of the child and what he imagines her doing (stanza 1) differ from the reality described in stanzas 2 and 3?
- Is the image presented in the last stanza imagined or real? To which of the images presented in the preceding stanzas of the poem is the one presented in the final stanza similar?
- Explain the literal and figurative meanings of 'her world of green' (line 9).
- What do lines 16–22 reveal about the persona of the poem?
- What do you think is meant by lines 39–41?

p.27 · *My Papa's Waltz*

- Why was the waltzing 'not easy' (line 4)?
- What do words like 'battered' (line 10), and 'scraped' (line 12) indicate about the waltz?
- What evidence is there in the poem that the persona enjoyed the waltzing?

p.28 · *Counter*

- The word 'counter' which is the title of the poem is repeated several times in the text of the poem. Examine the different contexts in which it is used and explain the meanings.
- Where do you suppose the 'second row' (lines 10 and 14) is?
- What is 'that distress' referred to in line 11?

p.28 · *Little Boy Crying*

- Who is the ogre referred to in line 8?
- Whose thoughts are reflected in stanza 2? Why does the poet use words like 'ogre' and 'giant' (line 8), and 'colossal' (line 9)?
- What is being alluded to in lines 11–13?
- How does the image of the adult presented in stanza 3 differ from that in stanza 2?

p.29 · *Coming Out*

'debutante' (line 12) – a young (upper class) woman who is formally introduced to society (at a social event, e.g. a dance). This event is sometimes referred to as a 'coming out'.

'card's marked' (line 18) – usually at debutante balls (dances) the ladies had cards with the list of dances on them. The men would 'book' a dance by putting their marks (e.g. their names) next to the dance that they wished to have with the young lady.

- What is happening in the poem/the event that is described?
- What is the purpose and effect of the 'observations' that are presented in stanzas 1 and 2?
- Who is the reluctant debutante?
- Discuss the effectiveness of the images of a ball to present the main event of the poem. You may consider, among others, phrases like 'blue frock', 'sequins', 'life's long ball', 'early dances'.

p.30 | *Early Innocence*

- Consider the contexts in which the words 'Remorse' (line 1), 'pure' (line 5) and 'Doubt' (line 10) occur and say what they indicate about the way in which the persona viewed the activities described.
- The poet suggests in stanza 5 that activities like the ones described lose their innocence in different situations. What are those situations?
- How do you interpret the last two lines of the poem?

p.31 | *Gull*

- Why does the poet use the word 'ungrateful' (line 5) to describe the gull?
- From the information that the poet presents, do you agree with his interpretation of the boy's action in lines 21–24?
- Do you agree with the views expressed in lines 30–40?

p.32 | *Childhood*

'roseapple tree' (line 4) – presumably the 'pomarosa' or pomerac, a fruit shaped like a pear with a vivid red skin, white pulp and round, web-covered seed.
'Job's Tears' (line 14) – a hardy, destructive grass that chokes other plants and bears green, black, white or grey seeds that can be strung into necklaces.

- Compare this poem with 'Early Innocence' by James Berry. Are there any similarities in the activities that the children are engaged in? In what ways do the respective poets differ in the treatment of the subject matter?

p.33 *Once Upon a Time*

- What things of childhood does the speaking voice of the poem wish for?
- What is implied about growing up and the life of adulthood?
- Can you suggest to whom 'they' and 'their' (lines 2, 4, etc.) refer? Is it made clear in the poem?
- Read lines 1–3 and lines 37–43 carefully. How do you interpret the meaning of these lines?

p.34 *River Girl*

'roostering' (line 11) – a rooster is a male fowl (a cock) that usually heralds the dawn with its crowing.
'constellation' (line 14) – a group of stars as seen from earth.

- The poem presents a thirteen-year-old boy's fascination/falling in love with a 'river girl'. Identify the phrases and images that emphasise his feelings.
- Comment on the image in the following lines 'the first frantic song of my blood/roostering my sleep of indifference' and discuss its significance in relation to the persona's experience.
- The moon and stars are important images in the poem. Discuss the poet's use of these images in the development of the theme of the poem.
- How would you describe the adult's recollection of the experience described in the poem?
- Comment on the following phrases in the final stanza of the poem: 'strong its stare', 'the heart of that moment', 'the stars dimmed', 'the river's fragments mended their vision'.
- What do you think are the 'rites' referred to in the last line of the poem?

p.35 *Forgive My Guilt*

- What is the sin the persona thinks he has 'done'?
- Why does he think it was a sin? Try to refer to specific words, phrases and/or lines in the poem to support your interpretation.
- How does the detailed description of the birds in lines 6–7 contrast with that in lines 11–12? What point in the poem do these descriptions help to emphasise?
- In your own words explain the meaning of lines 17–19.

PLACES

West Indies, U.S.A.

Cruising at thirty thousand feet above the endless green
the islands seem like dice tossed on a casino's baize,
some come up lucky, others not. Puerto Rico takes the pot,
the Dallas of the West Indies, silver linings on the clouds
5 as we descend are hall-marked, San Juan glitters
like a maverick's gold ring.

        All across the Caribbean
we'd collected terminals – airports are like calling cards,
cultural fingermarks; the hand-written signs at Port-
10 au-Prince, Piarco's sleazy tourist art, the lethargic
contempt of the baggage boys at 'Vere Bird' in St Johns . . .
And now for plush San Juan.

        But the pilot's bland,
you're safe in my hands drawl crackles as we land,
15 'US regulations demand all passengers not disembarking
at San Juan stay on the plane, I repeat, stay on the plane.'
Subtle Uncle Sam, afraid too many desperate blacks
might re-enslave this *I*sland of the free,
might jump the barbed

20   electric fence around 'America's
back yard' and claim that vaunted sanctuary . . . 'give me your poor . . .'
Through toughened, tinted glass the contrasts tantalise;
US patrol cars glide across the shimmering tarmac,
containered baggage trucks unload with fierce efficiency.
25 So soon we're climbing,

        low above the pulsing city streets;
galvanised shanties overseen by condominiums
polished Cadillacs shimmying past Rastas with pushcarts
and as we climb, San Juan's fools-glitter calls to mind
30 the shattered innards of a TV set that's fallen
off the back of a lorry, all painted valves and circuits
the roads like twisted wires,

        the bright cars, micro-chips.
It's sharp and jagged and dangerous, and belonged to someone else.

p.47 *Stewart Brown*

42

Geography Lesson

When the jet sprang into the sky,
it was clear why the city
had developed the way it had,
seeing it scaled six inches to the mile.
5   There seemed an inevitability
about what on ground had looked haphazard,
unplanned and without style
when the jet sprang into the sky.

When the jet reached ten thousand feet,
10   it was clear why the country
had cities where rivers ran
and why the valleys were populated.
The logic of geography –
that land and water attracted man –
15   was clearly delineated
when the jet reached ten thousand feet.

When the jet rose six miles high,
it was clear that the earth was round
and that it had more sea than land.
20   But it was difficult to understand
that the men on the earth found
causes to hate each other, to build
walls across cities and to kill.
From that height, it was not clear why.

p.47 *Zulfikar Ghose*

A View of Dingle Bay, Ireland

On a prowl for rhyme and reason, I jog
a secondary road between the farms
and there before me like the cantle of a saddle
lies the Bay of Dingle, compliments
5   of American Express and a god

who composes picture postcard views
across creation with indiscriminate
panache, from Caucasus to Caribbean,
from Lake Hakone to Victoria Falls,
10   and leaves it up to us which ones to choose.

From either flank low hills slope down
to a passage wide enough for Viking ships
or a tired dolphin flipping out for pay.
Under a Heaney 'freak of light' a field
15   brindles with cows. On my side is the town

and a pool-pocked strip of sand more littoral
than beach. Will this vista stir my pulse
or of romantic landscapes as with ghettos
can it reluctantly be said, 'If you
20   have seen one, you have seen them all.'

But surely that farmer in his Wellie boots
is the apotheosis of devotion
to the soil! His centuries of ploughing
sillions down could seed the earth. And is
25   his planting more than a putting down of roots?

p.47   *Ralph Thompson*

from The Emigrants

Columbus from his after-
deck watched stars, absorbed in water,
melt in liquid amber drifting

through my summer air.

5   Now with morning, shadows lifting,
beaches stretched before him cold and clear.

Birds circled flapping flag and mizzen

mast: birds harshly hawking, without fear,
Discovery he sailed for was so near.

10   Columbus from his after-

deck watched heights he hoped for,
rocks he dreamed, rise solid from my simple water.

Parrots screamed. Soon he would touch

our land, his charted mind's desire.
15   The blue sky blessed the morning with its fire.

But did his vision

fashion, as he watched the shore,
the slaughter that his soldiers

furthered here? Pike

20   point and musket butt,
hot splintered courage, bones

cracked with bullet shot,

tipped black boot in my belly, the
whip's uncurled desire?

25   Columbus from his after-

deck saw bearded fig trees, yellow pouis
blazed like pollen and thin

waterfalls suspended in the green

as his eyes climbed towards the highest ridges
30   where our farms were hidden.

Now he was sure

he heard soft voices mocking in the leaves.
What did this journey mean, this
new world mean? dis-
35   covery? Or a return to terrors
he had sailed from. Known before?

I watched him pause.

Then he was splashing silence.

Crabs snapped their claws
40 and scattered as he walked towards our shore.

p.48   *Kamau Brathwaite*

Sonnet Composed Upon Westminster Bridge, September 3, 1802

Earth has not anything to show more fair:
Dull would he be of soul who could pass by
A sight so touching in its majesty;
This City now doth, like a garment, wear
5 The beauty of the morning; silent, bare,
Ships, towers, domes, theatres, and temples lie
Open unto the fields, and to the sky;
All bright and glittering in the smokeless air.
Never did sun more beautifully steep
10 In his first splendour, valley, rock, or hill;
Ne'er saw I, never felt, a calm so deep!
The river glideth at his own sweet will:
Dear God! the very houses seem asleep;
And all that mighty heart is lying still!

p.48   *William Wordsworth*

Notes and questions

p.42

West Indies, U.S.A.

'baize' (line 2) – the green, felt-like material that usually covers gambling tables in casinos.

'hall-marked' (line 5) – a hall-mark is placed by manufacturers on objects made from precious metals.

'maverick' (line 6) – a rebellious, pleasure-seeking adventurer.

'condominiums' (line 27) – expensive apartments, often purchased by outsiders as holiday homes.

- What is the persona saying about the Caribbean by using the language and imagery of the gambling casino in stanza 1?

- The quotation 'give me your poor' (line 21) is from an inscription on the base of the Statue of Liberty overlooking the approaches to New York Harbor. What is the purpose of quoting it here?

- Note the way that the last line of the poem summarises the experience of the persona and pronounces a final judgement on it.

p.43

Geography Lesson

- Compare this poem with 'West Indies, U.S.A.' by Stewart Brown. In each poem the persona looks down upon the land from the window of an aeroplane. Note that, in both poems, this view or perspective helps the persona to see things about the place that it would be impossible to see from the ground.

- In this poem the persona's view makes clear for him several things that he did not understand about human civilization. But at the end of the poem we learn that there is one thing that is *not* made clear, no matter how high the plane goes. What is that one thing, and can you suggest a reason why?

p.43

A View of Dingle Bay, Ireland

'American Express' (line 5) – a credit company that issues credit cards on which people charge the goods and services they purchase and then repay the company (American Express) at a later date.

'panache' (line 8) – a dashing manner.

'Heaney' (line 14) – the name of another poet (Seamus Heaney).

'freak of light' (line 14) – a quotation from a poem by Heaney.

'littoral' (line 16) – relating to the shore of a sea, lake or ocean – a coastal or shore region.

'apotheosis' (line 22) – elevation to the rank of a god, or the glorification of a person or thing, or to idealise someone or something.

'sillions' (line 24) – furrows in ploughed fields.

- In lines 4 to 10 the poet says that a 'god' composes pictures/scenes of places across the world and leaves it up to 'us' to choose. Who is the 'us' that he refers to? What has the persona of the poem chosen?

- In lines 4 and 5 the persona says that he got his view with 'compliments of American Express'. What do you think he means by this? What is he doing in the poem?

- What is the point of the questions the persona asks in stanza 4?

- 'But surely' (stanza 5, line 21) indicates a change in the trend of thought. What is the point of the observation made in the last stanza?

p.44 | from *The Emigrants*

This poem is an imaginative reconstruction of the moment Columbus arrived and set foot in the new world.

- Who do you think is speaking in the poem, and how do you know?

- Why does the persona mention (lines 16–24) the death and destruction that do not occur until some time after this moment? How does this affect the mood of the poem?

- Why, in your opinion, does the poet make Columbus 'pause' in line 37?

p.46 | *Sonnet Composed Upon Westminster Bridge*

- What does the time of day (we are told that it is early morning) have to do with the type of scene depicted here?

- How do we know that the persona considers this particular perception of the city to be unusual?

- What is 'all that mighty heart' (line 14) and why is it lying still?

- In what way does the image of the 'heart' contrast with the imagery in the rest of the poem?

PEOPLE AND DESIRES

This picture illustrates the poem, 'It is the Constant Image of your Face', on page 85 in this section.

Liminal

evening
the late sky is rinsed of cloud
hills are shuddering lightly in a wind
drawing their ruffled burred coats a little tighter round them.
5   this time of day, this light
the mountains have stopped climbing
they seem to slope, heavy dark slumps of land
as though earth herself is letting go.
in the fold and groin and contour of her hills
10   the green is growing into dark
flowers dim, like freckles of a girl becoming woman, leaving
only hints of what they were, tinted on darkness
the veined sky tightens like a stretched skin
sunset dries out in daguerreotype.

15   since childhood i have done this
watched the day end and the night come
and tried to draw a line between them, isolate
the moment, hold it
with my will, the whole bent of my self
20   but i have never: now i seldom try.
still, without intending – following a felt urge –
i can't let many days go by
not watching the sun set.
i distrust the theories and book-answers that I've read on this
25   they may be right, but they may misconstrue me
i only wish mysterious evening light
would, one day, pour its darkening clarity through me.

p.74 *Kendel Hippolyte*

50

Naima

for John Coltrane

Propped against the crowded bar
he pours into the curved and silver horn
his old unhappy longing for a home

the dancers twist and turn
5   he leans and wishes he could burn
his memories to ashes like some old notorious emperor

of rome. but no stars blazed across the sky when he was born
no wise men found his hovel. this crowded bar
where dancers twist and turn

10   holds all the fame and recognition he will ever earn
on earth or heaven. he leans against the bar
and pours his old unhappy longing in the saxophone

p.74   **Kamau Brathwaite**

limbo-man

stick figure twining
for the tourist   then he marks
time, eyeing the linear link that bottles
his energies

5   a single
voice thrills: 'how low can you go?'

and the pelvic
girdle pulsates pulling
patrons

10   and the music
masters him
marshalls him into a one
dimensional strut

there he
15 goes, legs wide apart   inching
his way under
a borderline

p.74 *Judith Hamilton*

Coolie Mother

Jasmattie live in bruk –
Down hut big like Bata shoe-box,
Beat clothes, weed yard, chop wood, feed fowl
For this body and that body and every blasted body,
5 Fetch water, all day fetch water like if the whole –
Whole slow-flowing Canje river God create
Just for *she* one own bucket.

Till she foot-bottom crack and she hand cut-up
And curse swarm from she mouth like red-ants
10 And she cough blood on the ground but mash it in:
Because Jasmattie heart hard, she mind set hard.

To hustle save she one-one slow penny,
Because one-one dutty make dam cross the Canje
And she son Harilall *got* to go school in Georgetown,
15 *Must* wear clean starch pants, or they go laugh at he,
Strap leather on he foot, and he *must* read book,
Learn talk proper, take exam, go to England university,
Not turn out like he rum-sucker chamar dadee.

p.75 *David Dabydeen*

Coolie Son

(The Toilet Attendant Writes Home)

Taana boy, how you do?
How Shanti stay? And Sukhoo?
Mosquito still a-bite all-you?

Juncha dead true-true?
5 Mala bruk-foot set?
Food deh foh eat yet?

Englan nice, snow and dem ting,
A land dey say fit for a king,
Iceapple plenty on de tree and bird a-sing –
10 Is de beginning of what dey call 'The Spring'.

And I eating enough for all a-we
And reading book bad-bad.

But is what make Matam wife fall sick
And Sonnel cow suck dry wid tick?

15 Soon, I go turn lawya or dacta,
But, just now, passage money run out

So I tek lil wuk –
I is a Deputy Sanitary Inspecta,
Big-big office, boy! Tie round me neck!
20 Brand new uniform, one big bunch keys!
If Ma can see me now how she go please . . .

p.75 *David Dabydeen*

Mama Dot's Treatise

Mosquitoes
Are the fattest
Inhabitants
Of this republic.

5 They suck our blood
From the cradle
And flaunt it
Like a fat wallet.

They form dark
10 Haloes; we spend

Our outdoors
Dodging sainthood.

They force us
Into an all-night
15   Purdah of nets
Against them.

O to stop them
Milking us
Till we are bait
20   For worms;

Worms that don't
Know which way
To turn and will
Inherit the earth.

p.75   *Fred D'Aguiar*

The Carpenter's Complaint

Now you think that is right, sah? Talk the truth.
The man was mi friend. *I* build it, *I*
Build the house that him live in; but now
That him dead, that mawga-foot bwoy, him son,
5   Come say, him want a nice job for the coffin,
So him give it to *Mister* Belnavis to make –
That big-belly crook who don't know him arse
From a chisel, but because him is big-shot, because
Him make big-shot coffin, fi-him coffin must better
10   Than mine! Bwoy, it hot me, it hot me
For true. Fix we a nex' one, Miss Fergie –
That man coulda knock back him waters, you know sah!
I remember the day in this said-same bar
When him drink Old Brown and Coxs'n into
15   The ground, then stand up straight as a plumb-line
And keel him felt hat on him head and walk
Home cool, cool, cool. Dem was water-bird, brother!
Funeral? *Me*, sah? That bwoy have to learn
That a man have him pride. But bless mi days!

20   Good enough to make the house that him live in,
But not good enough to make him coffin!   *}irony*
I woulda do it for nutt'n, for nutt'n! The man
Was mi friend. Damn mawga-foot bwoy.
Is university turn him fool. I tell you,   →*irony*
25   It burn me, it burn me for true!

p.75   *Edward Baugh*

Swimming Chenango Lake

Winter will bar the swimmer soon.
  He reads the water's autumnal hesitations
A wealth of ways: it is jarred,
  It is astir already despite its steadiness,
5   Where the first leaves at the first
  Tremor of the morning air have dropped
Anticipating him, launching their imprints
  Outwards in eccentric, overlapping circles.
There is a geometry of water, for this
10   Squares off the clouds' redundances
And sets them floating in a nether atmosphere
  All angles and elongations: every tree
Appears a cypress as it stretches there
  And every bush that shows the season,
15   A shaft of fire. It is a geometry and not
  A fantasia of distorting forms, but each
Liquid variation answerable to the theme
  It makes away from, plays before:
It is a consistency, the grain of the pulsating flow.
20   But he has looked long enough, and now
Body must recall the eye to its dependence
  As he scissors the waterscape apart
And sways it to tatters. Its coldness
  Holding him to itself, he grants the grasp,
25   For to swim is also to take hold
  On water's meaning, to move in its embrace
And to be, between grasp and grasping free.
  He reaches in-and-through to that space
The body is heir to, making a where

30   In water, a possession to be relinquished
Willingly at each stroke. The image he has torn
    Flows-to behind him, healing itself,
Lifting and lengthening, splayed like the feathers
    Down an immense wing whose darkened spread
35 Shadows his solitariness: alone, he is unnamed
    By this baptism, where only Chenango bears a name
In a lost language he begins to construe –
A speech of densities and derisions, of half-
Replies to the questions his body must frame
40   Frogwise across the all but penetrable element.
Human, he fronts it and, human, he draws back
    From the interior cold, the mercilessness
That yet shows a kind of mercy sustaining him.
    The last sun of the year is drying his skin
45 Above a surface a mere mosaic of tiny shatterings,
    Where a wind is unscaping all images in the flowing obsidian,
The going-elsewhere of ripples incessantly shaping.

p.75   *Charles Tomlinson*

Cold as Heaven

Before there is a breeze again
before the cooling days of Lent, she may be gone.
My grandmother asks me to tell her
again about the snow.
5 We sit on her white bed
in this white room, while outside
the Caribbean sun winds up the world
like an old alarm clock. I tell her
about the enveloping blizzard I lived through
10 that made everything and everyone the same;
how we lost ourselves in drifts so tall
we fell through our own footprints;
how wrapped like mummies in layers of wool
that almost immobilized us, we could only
15 take hesitant steps like toddlers
toward food, warmth, shelter.
I talk winter real for her,

as she would once conjure for me to dream
at sweltering siesta time,
20   cool stone castles in lands far north.
Her eyes wander to the window,
to the teeming scene of children
pouring out of a yellow bus, then to the bottle
dripping minutes through a tube
25   into her veins. When her eyes return to me,
I can see she's waiting to hear more
about the purifying nature of ice,
how snow makes way for a body,
how you can make yourself an angel
30   by just lying down and waving your arms
as you do when you say
good-bye.

p.76   *Judith Ortiz Cofer*

Corruption

A young clerk peruses the court's files.
Somewhere along the table, a fly zzzzz past with the car's horns
blaring outside

The young clerk is tense;
5   that image of a pregnant wife
lying
painfully
hungrily
at the Ocean Road Hospital bed
10   whispers something in his heart's ears

'Destroy the file for me' zooms the rapacious voice
of the big-bellied man who just left him a while ago;
the appeal limps in his veins
waving a flag of those red-pinkish 1,000 shillings notes

15   no more pains
no more taxi-worries
the mother shall carry the new-born baby home
comfortably

Suddenly the court's file is in shreds.
20   Its white smiling pieces laugh loudly
applauding
the wish
of the rich bureaucrat
that has just been
25   implemented

p.76 *Freddy Macha*

Richard Cory

Whenever Richard Cory went down town,
We people on the pavement looked at him:
He was a gentleman from sole to crown,
Clean favored, and imperially slim.

5   And he was always quietly arrayed,
And he was always human when he talked;
But still he fluttered pulses when he said,
'Good-morning,' and he glittered when he walked.

And he was rich – yes, richer than a king –
10   And admirably schooled in every grace:
In fine, we thought that he was everything
To make us wish that we were in his place.

So on we worked, and waited for the light,
And went without the meat, and cursed the bread;
15   And Richard Cory, one calm summer night,
Went home and put a bullet through his head.

p.76 *Edwin Arlington Robinson*

The Teacher

Why do I forget question marks.
I am notorious for it.
My students scoff at me,
'How can you teach English when
5   you don't punctuate proper?'

I don't teach you anyway, I think,
just lead you like a scout master
and hope you'll dip your hand
into the brook – cold like no
10 tap water you've ever felt,
let you marvel, a little frightened,
at a snake, mouth agape,
before it darts between rocks,
an image you'll carry for years,
15 spur you to anger when I won't
stop to let you rest,
even hope you catch poison ivy,
and, as we race up the hill,
urge you on when
20 you leave me behind,
gasping,
a seeming spear
wedged between my ribs.

Of the absent question mark, I say,
25 'An innocent, harmless error,'
And those of you who aren't smug
point out that I should
extend to you
the same courteous understanding.
30 I uncap my canteen,
drop to the grass, and,
before I take a long swig,
say, 'Why not.'

p.76   *Tom Romano*

59

Ancestors (Part I)

Every Friday morning my grandfather
left his farm of canefields, chickens, cows,
and rattled in his trap down to the harbour town
to sell his meat. He was a butcher.
5   Six-foot-three and very neat: high collar,
winged, a grey cravat, a waistcoat, watch-
chain just above the belt, thin narrow-
bottomed trousers, and the shoes his wife
would polish every night. He drove the trap
10 himself: slap of the leather reins
along the horse's back and he'd be off
with a top-hearted homburg on his head:
black English country gentleman.

Now he is dead. The meat shop burned,
15 his property divided. A doctor bought
the horse. His mad alsatians killed it.
The wooden trap was chipped and chopped
by friends and neighbours and used to stop-
gap fences and for firewood. One yellow
20 wheel was rolled across the former cowpen gate.
Only his hat is left. I 'borrowed' it.
I used to try it on and hear the night wind
man go battering through the canes, cocks waking up and thinking
it was dawn throughout the clinking country night.
25 Great caterpillar tractors clatter down
the broken highway now; a diesel engine grunts
where pigs once hunted garbage.
A thin asthmatic cow shares the untrashed garage.

p.77   *Kamau Brathwaite*

Silk Cotton Trees

Secrets of centuries clutched
within their gnarled trunks.

They are silent seers
of ancestors, backs bent in blazing sun,
5   seeding earth to birth young trees,
the backbone of a nation.

When, in the noonday heat,
some girl, shunning the overseer's
pulsing whip, would hide
10   in foliage at their feet

their branches bent
to mark the place where she,
holding within her breast the memory
of one who gave himself to shield her
15   from the hurt of that same whip,
fell to the whim of massa's will.

There in the darkening earth
she buried one stillborn
between the roots.

20   Now the ghosts of all those loves
whose hearts were given, taken, broken
in that place
sigh the wind's silken breath
through the leaves of these
25   silk cotton trees.

p.77 *Hazel Simmons-McDonald*

Drought

The woman is barren. And the blackbirds
have had a hard time this year with the drought
and fallen like moths to the field's floor.

The woman is barren. And the city,
5   crawling south like an oil-slick
will soon be around her ankles.

So she sings: 'Will you marry me?
I will go searching under many flat stones
for moisture of the departed rains.'

10   Sings: O world, will you marry me?

The riverbed's dried up completely, the lizards
have taken to the trees, to the high branches.
The cane rolls westwards, burning burning

In the sunset of her time, in the ploughed crater
15 where the woman like a frail apostrophe
dances palely each evening

Among the fallen blackbirds.

p.77 *Wayne Brown*

Revelation

Turn sideways now and let them see
What loveliness escapes the schools,
Then turn again, and smile, and be
The perfect answer to those fools
5 Who always prate of Greece and Rome,
'The face that launched a thousand ships,'
And such like things, but keep tight lips
For burnished beauty nearer home.
Turn in the sun, my love, my love!
10 What palm-like grace! What poise! I swear
I prize these dusky limbs above my life.
What laughing eyes! What gleaming hair!

p.77 *H. A. Vaughan*

Man with a Hook

This man I
know (about a year
ago, when he was young) blew
his arm off in the cellar
5 making bombs
to explode the robins
on the lawns.

Now he has a hook
instead of a hand;

10 It is an ingenious
gadget, and comes
with various attachments:
knife for meals,
pink plastic hand for everyday
15 handshakes, black stuffed leather glove
for social functions.

I attempt pity

But, Look, he says, glittering
like a fanatic. My hook
20 is an improvement:

      and to demonstrate
lowers his arm: the steel question-
mark turns and opens,
and from his burning
25 cigarette
        unscrews
and holds the delicate
ash: a thing
precise
30 my clumsy tender-
skinned pink fingers
couldn't do.

p.77 **_Margaret Atwood_**

I Knew a Woman

I knew a woman, lovely in her bones,
When small birds sighed, she would sigh back at them;
Ah, when she moved, she moved more ways than one:
The shapes a bright container can contain!
5 Of her choice virtues only gods should speak,
Or English poets who grew up on Greek
(I'd have them sing in chorus, cheek to cheek).

How well her wishes went! She stroked my chin,
She taught me Turn, and Counter-turn, and Stand;
10 She taught me Touch, that undulant white skin;
I nibbled meekly from her proffered hand;
She was the sickle; I, poor I, the rake,
Coming behind her for her pretty sake
(But what prodigious mowing we did make).

15 Love likes a gander, and adores a goose:
Her full lips pursed, the errant note to seize;
She played it quick, she played it light and loose;
My eyes, they dazzled at her flowing knees;
Her several parts could keep a pure repose,
20 Or one hip quiver with a mobile nose
(She moved in circles, and those circles moved).

Let seed be grass, and grass turn into hay:
I'm martyr to a motion not my own;
What's freedom for? To know eternity.
25 I swear she cast a shadow white as stone.
But who would count eternity in days?
These old bones live to learn her wanton ways:
(I measure time by how a body sways).

p.78 **Theodore Roethke**

Orchids

I leave this house
box pieces of the five-week life I've gathered.

I'll send them on
to fill spaces in my future life.

5 One thing is left
a spray of orchids someone gave
from a bouquet one who
makes a ritual of flower-giving sent.

The orchids have no fragrance
10 but purple petals draw you
to look at the purple heart.

I watered them once
when the blossoms were full blown
like polished poems.
15 I was sure they'd wilt
and I would toss them out with the five-week litter.

They were stubborn.
I starved them.
They would not die.

20 This morning the bud at the stalk's tip unfurled.

I think I'll pluck the full-blown blooms
press them between pages of memory.

Perhaps in their thin dried transparency

I'll discover their peculiar poetry.

p78 *Hazel Simmons-McDonald*

God's Work

Mister Edwards, more my good friend
Than gardener and handyman at home,
Served me well for half my life.
Prince, they called him, born about that colonial time:
5 I called him Mister Edwards until the hour he died.

Strong black face, handsome old man,
Ashy cap of curled short hair,
Never sick a day until a day he sick.
'Wind by the heart', he said
10 But the heart was sound, too sound,
It took months of agony to kill him
Ripping his guts away slowly
Until that strong, good man was nothing.

'God's work', he would say
15 When the rain pelted down
And floods rushed in the rivers
And storms lashed the tree-tops.

And 'God's work' now he said
When the pain wracked him
20   Spasms crumpling up his face
Sweat dripping in the effort to hold back
The gut-contracting cry not quite escaping.
'Prince Edwards, he too strong for cry',
But his last day in my arms he cried.
25   'God's work!'
God should play more.

p.78 *Ian McDonald*

La belle qui fut . . .

Miss Rossignol lived in the lazaretto
For Roman Catholic crones; she had white skin,
And underneath it, fine, old-fashioned bones;
She flew like bats to vespers every twilight,
5   The living Magdalen of Donatello;
And tipsy as a bottle when she stalked
On stilted legs to fetch the morning milk,
In a black shawl harnessed by rusty brooches.
My mother warned us how that flesh knew silk
10   Coursing a green estate in gilded coaches.
While Miss Rossignol, in the cathedral loft
Sang to her one dead child, a tattered saint
Whose pride had paupered beauty to this witch
Who was so fine once, whose hands were so soft.

p.78 *Derek Walcott*

Girl Reporter

Fact is her fiction. Sitting in the bar
Raincoat still on, crossed nylon legs revealing
Less than we think, a male in tow and smiling –
Her narrowed eyes flick past to register
5   Whether I am a story in the offing.

Life is material for her creation.
The doll by the up-turned scooter – that is real,
Its head, see, stains the kerb. She runs to call
The news-desk first, then after the police-station,
10   Already mapping the story of the trial.

Errors of fact are part of her prose style.
With every slashing cross-head some truth dies.
In love? She knows. You hate her? She knows. You'll
Cure cancer? reach the moon? Her face may smile –
15   You're placed by those all-knowing know-all eyes.

What chance has truth against such showy error?
We're butterflies pinned down by this young lady,
Facts of our lives are melted down for cliché.
Even as I write her gaze observes my tremor –
20   Her lethal pencil always at the ready.

p.79   *Philip Hobsbaum*

The Woman Speaks to the Man who has Employed her Son

Her son was first made known to her
as a sense of unease, a need to cry
for little reasons and a metallic tide
rising in her mouth each morning.
5   Such signs made her know
that she was not alone in her body.
She carried him full term
tight up under her heart

She carried him like the poor
10   carry hope, hope you get a break
or a visa, hope one child go through
and remember you. He had no father.
The man she made him with had more
like him, he was fair-minded
15   he treated all his children
with equal and unbiased indifference.

She raised him twice, once as mother
then as father, set no ceiling
on what he could be doctor,
20 earth healer, pilot take wings.
But now he tells her he is working
for you, that you value him so much
you give him one whole submachine gun
for him alone.

25 He says you are like a father to him
she is wondering what kind of father
would give a son hot and exploding
death, when he asks him for bread.
She went downtown and bought three
30 and one-third yards of black cloth
and a deep crowned and veiled hat
for the day he draw his bloody salary.

She has no power over you and this
at the level of earth, what she has
35 are prayers and a mother's tears
and at knee city she uses them.
She says psalms for him
she reads psalms for you
she weeps for his soul
40 her eyewater covers you.

She is throwing a partner
with Judas Iscariot's mother
the thief on the left-hand side
of the cross, his mother
45 is the banker, her draw though
is first and last for she still
throwing two hands as mother and father.
She is prepared, she is done. Absalom.

p.79 *Lorna Goodison*

In the New World

There is my uncle
pulling the new Dodge to the side
of the road, first in a family
of ox drivers to drive a car.
5   He is a farmer. It is
the only living thing he knows
how to exact from this new earth.
He is taking his corn and eggs
to market over clear, paved road.

10   Next to him, my aunt
in a checkered housedress
peers out through the same
wide window. Their daughter
is in back, the bright
15   sixteen-year-old they dote on,
an American. My uncle and aunt
are thin and grey as dust.
They have poured all their color
into her: red health, the grain shade
20   of her hair, green eyes
open to all they can contain.

What has happened
is a flat tire, some puncture
of the usual. My uncle
25   will jack up the ton of metal
with his own strength
and clever new tools. He is
an upright man, student of God
all his days. Everything waits
30   for him to hold it up. Behind them
someone doesn't see my uncle
pull up along the curve.
Suddenly, nothing will take them
any further. The child is dead,
35   the farm lost. The woman
must walk in pain all her life.
For years my uncle sits
more still than anyone,
hands locked between his knees.

Elaine Terranova

p 79

Apartment Neighbours

I never see them
yet our lives are linked
by more than walls

the faceless melody
5   of snores of man or mate
the several callers
marked by urgent knock
or crisp sound of rejected foot-
falling on hard paths
10 grass has never known

tinkle of glass
and plates that settle into sinks
swishing the running kitchen water

hiss of the muted phone
15 and late at night
too late
loud hoses washing
whining pet dogs
coaxing with tender tones
20 humaning them
there in our common backyard space
I cannot see

without them seeing me
and forcing me to smile
25 make a connection
break from the learned restraint
I wear in foreign lands

They never see me
yet I long to ease
30 my constant frown
and say
'Evening Miss Evvy, Miss Maisie
Miss Maud . . .'

p.79   ***Velma Pollard***

For my Mother (May I Inherit Half her Strength)

My mother loved my father
I write this as an absolute
in this my thirtieth year
the year to discard absolutes

5   he appeared, her fate disguised,
as a sunday player in a cricket match,
he had ridden from a country
one hundred miles south of hers.

She tells me he dressed the part,
10   visiting dandy, maroon blazer
cream serge pants, seam like razor,
and the beret and the two-tone shoes.

My father stopped to speak to her sister,
till he looked and saw her by the oleander,
15   sure in the kingdom of my blue-eyed grandmother.
He never played the cricket that day.

He wooed her with words and he won her.
He had nothing but words to woo her,
On a visit to distant Kingston he wrote,
20   'I stood on the corner of King Street and looked,
and not one woman in that town was lovely as you'.

My mother was a child of the petite bourgeoisie
studying to be a teacher, she oiled her hands to hold pens.
My father barely knew his father, his mother died young,
25   he was a boy who grew with his granny.

My mother's trousseau came by steamer through the snows
of Montreal
where her sisters Albertha of the cheekbones and the
perennial Rose, combed Jewlit backstreets with French-
30   turned names for Doris' wedding things.

Such a wedding Harvey River, Hanover, had never seen
Who anywhere had seen a veil fifteen chantilly yards long?
and a crepe de chine dress with inlets of silk godettes
and a neck-line clasped with jewelled pins!

35   And on her wedding day she wept. For it was a brazen bride in those days
who smiled.
and her bouquet looked for the world like a sheaf of wheat
against the unknown of her belly,
a sheaf of wheat backed by maidenhair fern, representing Harvey River
40   her face washed by something other than river water.

My father made one assertive move, he took the imported cherub down
from the heights of the cake and dropped it in the soft territory
between her breasts . . . and she cried.

When I came to know my mother many years later, I knew her as the figure
45   who sat at the first thing I learned to read: 'SINGER', and she breast-fed
my brother while she sewed; and she taught us to read while she sewed and
she sat in judgement over all our disputes as she sewed.

She could work miracles, she would make a garment from a square of cloth
in a span that defied time. Or feed twenty people on a stew made from
50   fallen-from-the-head cabbage leaves and a carrot and a cho-cho and a
                                                palmful
of meat. •

And she rose early and sent us clean into the world and she went to bed in
the dark, for my father came in always last.

There is a place somewhere where my mother never took the younger ones
55   a country where my father with the always smile
my father whom all women loved, who had the perpetual quality of
                                              wonder
given only to a child . . . hurt his bride.

Even at his death there was this 'Friend' who stood by her side,
but my mother is adamant that that has no place in the memory of
60   my father.

When he died, she sewed dark dresses for the women amongst us
and she summoned that walk, straight-backed, that she gave to us
and buried him dry-eyed.

Just that morning, weeks after
65   she stood delivering bananas from their skin
singing in that flat hill country voice

she fell down a note to the realization that she did
not have to be brave, just this once
and she cried.

70   For her hands grown coarse with raising nine children
for her body for twenty years permanently fat
for the time she pawned her machine for my sister's
Senior Cambridge fees
and for the pain she bore with the eyes of a queen

75   and she cried also because she loved him.

p.80   **Lorna Goodison**

Notes and questions

These poems bear witness to the variety within our human community and to our abiding interest in the human personality. In some poems the focus is upon the job or profession of the person; there are representations of teachers, musicians, postmen, gardeners and journalists. Some of the poems look at old people, some at black people, some at parents and some at strange, quirky people, like Margaret Atwood's 'Man with a Hook'.

p.50 *Liminal*

Title: 'liminal' – refers to the threshold between two worlds or states of being; in this case daylight and darkness.
'daguerreotype' (line 14) – an early type of photograph in which an impression was taken upon a silver plate sensitized by iodine and developed by mercury vapour. The process and the photograph are named after their French inventor Louis Daguerre.

- Note that the first part of the poem (lines 1–14) is an attempt to capture in detail the process of night enveloping the landscape; while the second part (lines 15–27) explains the persona's motive and his fascination for this process.

- Attempt to explain what the last two lines of the poem mean.

p.51 *Naima*

This poem is dedicated to John Coltrane, a celebrated jazz saxophonist, who is also the subject of the poem.

- What details tell us that the subject has had a hard life?

- What is the relationship between the music he plays and the type of life he has had?

- Is the poet talking only about the specific individual?

p.51 *limbo-man*

- What are some of the motives or incentives the limbo-man has for dancing?

- What are some of the things suggested by the last word of the poem?

p.52

Coolie Mother

'one-one dutty make dam' (line 13) – literally 'it takes one small spadeful of dirt at a time to build a dam', a Guyanese proverb which means that the slow accumulation of things over time eventually results in plenty.
'chamar' (line 18) – a low caste Hindu, used here as a term of abuse, the equivalent of 'worthless'.

- Explain in your own words why the mother is making all these sacrifices for her son.

p.52

Coolie Son

- Notice how the poem's sub-title makes the persona's boasts in the final stanza ironic.
- Why does the persona think he can get away with twisting the truth?
- What do you feel about the persona at the end of the poem? Should the fact that he shows real concern for the plight of friends and relatives back home rescue him from your condemnation?
- Point out some of the ironies that are generated when this poem is considered together with 'Coolie Mother'.

p.53

Mama Dot's Treatise

- What does the poet mean by 'dodging sainthood' in line 12?
- 'Purdah' (line 15) refers to the system of screening the faces of Hindu and Muslim women behind a veil for reasons of modesty. What does the word refer to in its context in the poem?
- What does it mean when the persona says that 'worms . . . will inherit the earth' (stanza 6)?

p.54

The Carpenter's Complaint

- Point out the details that suggest that the carpenter is talking in a familiar setting and to familiar company.
- Say in your own words why the carpenter is so hard on the dead man's son. Do you agree with his judgement?
- Notice how effectively the poet uses the Jamaican dialect in this poem. Point out some of the positive effects of this use of language.

p.55

Swimming Chenango Lake

Title: 'Chenango Lake' – a lake in New York State near Colgate University, where the poet, Tomlinson, taught in 1967. The poem is meant, Tomlinson once explained, to echo the ritual and ceremonies of native American Indians when they had to cross water. It is about the difference between looking at the water (the mask, the lake) and actually swimming in it (where the mask is removed and the water is experienced more fully).

- 'To swim is also to take hold on water's meaning' (lines 25–26). Which of the five senses, would you say, is most involved in this process?
- What, if anything, strikes you about the description of the action of swimming in lines 28–33: is this how one normally thinks of swimming? What is the reason for the poet's emphases and presentation of details here?

p.56 ## Cold as Heaven

- The poet is from Cuba, which is probably the setting of the poem. Quote two brief passages in the poem that indicate this setting.
- What is the purpose, given the above, of all the references to snow and cold?
- It seems that the persona's grandmother is expected to die soon. How is this reflected in the ending (the last four lines) of the poem?

p.57 ## Corruption

- What does the buzzing fly in line 2 contribute to the poem?
- Say in your own words what motivates the young man to destroy the file.
- How do you feel about the man who wants the file destroyed? Point out some of the words used to describe him that help you to assess his character.

p.58 ## Richard Cory

This is a poem about the deceptiveness of appearances and the danger of pre-judgement (prejudice).

- What are some of the qualities admired in Richard Cory?
- Can you suggest a reason why Richard Cory killed himself?
- What techniques does the poet use to ensure that Cory's death is as great a surprise for the reader as it is for his admirers in the poem?

p.59 ## The Teacher

- For most of this poem the teacher speaks of his role as that of a scoutmaster, taking the children on a hike. In what ways can this be seen as an appropriate metaphor for teaching in the classroom?

- Why do you think the teacher is willing to forgive the children their inattention to small details like the question mark? Do you agree with him?

Ancestors (Part I)

p.60

'trap' (line 3) – a small, two-wheeled, horse-drawn carriage.

- Consider the contrast between the two stanzas of this poem. Why is the change so devastating?
- What does the poem tell us about our attitude to the past?
- Why do we need to think at all about our ancestors? What can such thoughts have to do with our life in the present?

Silk Cotton Trees

p.60

'gnarled' (line 2) – twisted, knotted, covered with bumps.
'seers' (line 3) – 'those who see', with the suggestion of seeing into the future and the past.

- Relate in your own words the three instances (to be found in stanzas 3, 4 and 5) of the girl's involvement with the silk cotton tree.
- Is the poem really about trees or about history – and whose history?

Drought

p.61

- In what way is the woman in the poem like the drought?
- Why does she want to get married?
- Is she a real woman, do you think, and does it matter?

Revelation

p.62

'the face that launched a thousand ships' (line 6) – this is a reference to Helen of Troy, reputed to have been the most beautiful woman in the world, whose abduction from her Greek husband, King Menelaus, by the Trojan Paris caused the Greeks to sail to war against Troy.

- Who are 'those fools' referred to in line 4, and why does the poet denounce them?

Man with a Hook

p.62

- Why do you think the man is described as having been young 'a year ago' (lines 2–3)?
- Do you think the hook is really an improvement?
- What do his attitude and actions tell us about this man?

p.63 | *I Knew a Woman*

- This is a complex poem full of humorous qualifications and words and phrases that have more than one meaning. Note how the final lines (in brackets) of each stanza tend to alter or adjust our perspective of what has gone before.

- Words such as 'rake', 'goose' and 'loose' have connotations (suggested meanings) that are different from their literal meaning. These help construct an undercurrent of sensual/sexual suggestiveness in this poem. Point out two other words or phrases that contribute to that effect.

p.64 | *Orchids*

- Orchids are rare and highly prized flowers that mostly grow as parasites on other trees. Why do you think the persona compares or associates them with poems?

- . . . 'press them between pages of memory' (line 22) refers to the (now rare) habit of pressing flowers by flattening and drying them between the pages of heavy books. What, according to the poem's last two lines, does the poet hope to achieve by this action?

p.65 | *God's Work*

- What does his repeated phrase 'God's work' tell us about Prince Edwards?

- Why does the persona say at the end: 'God should play more' (line 26)?

- Compare 'God's Work' with the poem 'Amerindian' by Ian McDonald in Section Four: *From Time to Eternity* and comment on the circumstances of the death of the subject in each case.

p.66 | *La belle qui fut . . .*

Title: French for 'The beauty that was'.

This poem tells of the faded wealth, beauty and privilege of old Miss Rossignol who now lives as a pauper in an old ladies' home.

'the living Magdalen of Donatello' (line 5) – a sculpture of Mary Magdalen by Donatello, the 14th-century Florentine master.

- Note the way the poet paints a very clear and detailed picture of her physical appearance. Describe in your own words what she looks like.

- What is meant or suggested by 'fine, old-fashioned bones' (line 3)?

- What is the persona's attitude towards Miss Rossignol?

p.66

Girl Reporter

- Is the girl in this poem a 'good' reporter? Point out the details in the poem that help you decide.

- Describe in your own words the incident referred to in stanza 2. What details in this stanza give us a negative impression of the girl?

- What is ironic about the reference (line 19) to the persona writing the poem?

p.67

The Woman Speaks to the Man who has Employed her Son

'throwing a partner' (line 41) – a method of informal saving, widely practised throughout the Caribbean, where a number of people pay a fixed sum of money each month for a fixed period, with a different member of the group taking the collected total ('drawing a hand') each time.

- What is the 'work' that the son is doing?

- What is the purpose of the first three stanzas which describe the mother's struggle to give birth to the son and to raise him?

- What is meant by the phrases 'bloody salary' (line 32) and 'knee city' (line 36)?

- 'Absalom' (line 48) was the son of biblical King David who, under the influence of the traitor Achitophel, plotted against his father and was killed, causing the king profound grief. How is reference to this appropriate at this point in the poem?

p.69

In the New World

- As in 'The Woman Speaks to the Man who has Employed her Son', by Lorna Goodison, the parents in this poem have invested an entire life in their daughter who is killed in the car crash. Do you think the pain is greater here because the death is unexpected?

- 'American' (line 16) – the setting of the poem is Puerto Rico and the child was born after the island became an American Associate State; she is therefore an American citizen. How does this add to the pride and expectations of the parents?

p.70

Apartment Neighbours

- This poem describes the strain brought on by the enforced proximity of apartment-living in foreign countries. Point out two references to this sense of discomfort.

- Why is the appeal to the auditory imagination (the sense of hearing) so prominent in this poem?
- How does the life described here contrast with life in the Caribbean? (Note the final two lines which are a quote from a poem by Kamau Brathwaite, 'The Dust'.)

p.71 *For my Mother (May I Inherit Half her Strength)*

In this poem the poet celebrates her mother's life and marriage and the strength of her character which sustained the family throughout.

- Describe in your own words the characters of the mother and of the father. Why do you think the mother is stronger?
- How do you think the father 'hurt' his wife? How do you know?
- Name some of the qualities in the mother that the persona admires and would like to inherit.

LOVE

The Lady's-Maid's Song

When Adam found his rib was gone
He cursed and sighed and cried and swore,
And looked with cold resentment on
The creature God had used it for.
5 All love's delights were quickly spent
And soon his sorrow multiplied;
He learned to blame his discontent
On something stolen from his side.

And so in every age we find
10 Each Jack, destroying every Joan,
Divides and conquers womankind
In vengeance for the missing bone;
By day he spins out quaint conceits
With gossip, flattery and song
15 And then at night, between the sheets
He wrongs the girl to right the wrong.

Though shoulder, bosom, lip and knee
Are praised in every kind of art,
Here is Love's true anatomy:
20 His rib is gone; he'll have her heart.
So women bear the debt alone
And live eternally distressed,
For though we throw the dog his bone
He wants it back with interest.

p.88 *John Hollander*

Departure Lounge

The young man,
when the flight is called,
is blowing his nose to clear
the sadness of departure.

5 The girl who's leaving looks
composed. They're travelling
on different planes
to different destinations.

Each time
10 we die a little.
When we are young
these moments
devastate.

But partings down the years
15 have helped to make me
ready to say goodbye.

p.88 *Mervyn Morris*

Koriabo

Once in rainy season
When sky and river are one
I pause and smell your rank breath
Borne on the wet breeze,
5 And I shiver at the whisper it conveyed
Of your age and life and longing.
You whose vast memory
I enter, perhaps as a recent, ephemeral blur,
The touch of boat or body
10 Hardly registering, as I watch the wind
Blow across your wet back
Causing goosebumps of exploding raindrops,
And I think it is such a love
– And expressed like that –
15 That I long for.
I exhale audibly
(A gesture lost in the love-song of the rain)
And resume paddling.
I'm comforted by the perception
20 That, like you and the wind

And the rain, I have somewhere
To go. And who can say
That the love that I find
At the inscrutable end of my journey
25 Will not be as shiveringly perfect
As that cold kiss of the wind
On your bare, brown back?

p.88   *Mark McWatt*

Sonnet 73

That time of year thou mayst in me behold
When yellow leaves, or none, or few, do hang
Upon those boughs which shake against the cold,
Bare ruined choirs, where late the sweet birds sang.
5 In me thou see'st the twilight of such day
As after sunset fadeth in the west;
Which by and by black night doth take away,
Death's second self, that seals up all in rest.
In me thou see'st the glowing of such fire,
10 That on the ashes of his youth doth lie,
As the deathbed whereon it must expire,
Consumed with that which it was nourished by.
This thou perceiv'st, which makes thy love more strong,
To love that well which thou must leave ere long.

p.88   *William Shakespeare*

Lullaby

Lay your sleeping head, my love,
Human on my faithless arm;
Time and fevers burn away
Individual beauty from
5 Thoughtful children, and the grave
Proves the child ephemeral:
But in my arms till break of day

Let the living creature lie,
Mortal, guilty, but to me
10 The entirely beautiful.

Soul and body have no bounds:
To lovers as they lie upon
Her tolerant enchanted slope
In their ordinary swoon.
15 Grave the vision Venus sends
Of supernatural sympathy,
Universal love and hope;
While an abstract insight wakes
Among the glaciers and the rocks
20 The hermit's sensual ecstasy.

Certainty, fidelity
On the stroke of midnight pass
Like vibrations of a bell,
And fashionable madmen raise
25 Their pedantic boring cry:
Every farthing of the cost,
All the dreaded cards foretell,
Shall be paid, but from this night
Not a whisper, not a thought,
30 Not a kiss nor look be lost.

Beauty, midnight, vision dies:
Let the winds of dawn that blow
Softly round your dreaming head
Such a day of sweetness show
35 Eye and knocking heart may bless,
Find the mortal world enough;
Noons of dryness see you fed
By the involuntary powers,
Nights of insult let you pass
40 Watched by every human love.

p.89 *W. H. Auden*

Hate

Hate swelled up inside me,
Choking me, strangling me,
Hiding me from myself behind it.
I could only stand and watch me as I bellowed and shouted at my friend.

5   I heard me abuse him,
Poison others against him
And do many despicable things.
Then myself forced its way through
And I shook hands and said I was sorry.

10   Hate is a funny thing;
It splits you in two,
One part against the other,
So that you can never win.

p.89 *David Eva (aged 13)*

It is the Constant Image of your Face

It is the constant image of your face
framed in my hands as you knelt before my chair
the grave attention of your eyes
surveying me amid my world of knives
5   that stays with me, perennially accuses
and convicts me of heart's-treachery;
and neither you nor I can plead excuses
for you, you know, can claim no loyalty –
my land takes precedence of all my loves.

10   Yet I beg mitigation, pleading guilty
for you, my dear, accomplice of my heart
made, without words, such blackmail with your beauty
and proffered me such dear protectiveness
that I confess without remorse or shame
15   my still-fresh treason to my country
and hope that she, my other, dearest love
will pardon freely, not attaching blame
being your mistress (or your match) in tenderness.

p.89 *Dennis Brutus*

Light Love

I, remembering how light love
hath a soft footfall, and fleet
that goes clicking down
the heart's lone
5   and empty street
in a kind
of spread twilight-nimbus of the mind,
and a soft voice of shaken laughter
like the wind . . .

10   I, remembering this,
And remembering that light love is
As fragile as a kiss
Lightly given,
And passes like the little rain
15   softly down-driven . . .

Bade love come to you
with rough male footsteps –
Deliberate –
That hurt to come,
20   And hurt to go . . .

And bade love speak to you
With accents terrible, and slow.

p.89   *Roger Mais*

Silver Wedding

The party is over and I sit among
The flotsam that its passing leaves,
The dirty glasses and fag-ends:
Outside, a black wind grieves.

5   Two decades and a half of marriage;
It does not really seem as long,
And yet I find I have scant knowledge
Of youth's ebullient song.

David, my son, my loved rival,
10   And Julia, my tapering daughter,
Now grant me one achievement only:
I turn their wine to water.

And Helen, partner of all these years,
Helen, my spouse, my sack of sighs,
15   Reproaches me for every hurt
With injured, bovine eyes.

There must have been passion once, I grant,
But neither she nor I could bear
To have its ghost come prowling from
20   Its dark and frowsy lair.

And we, to keep our nuptials warm,
Still wage sporadic, fire-side war;
Numb with insult each yet strives
To scratch the other raw.

25   Twenty-five years we've now survived;
I'm not sure either why or how
As I sit with a wreath of quarrels set
On my tired and balding brow.

p.90   **Vernon Scannell**

Notes and questions

The poems in this section deal with different forms and manifestations of love and the relationships in which it is expressed. Several themes associated with love are explored. It may be helpful to make a summary statement that expresses what each poem is about, the theme(s) explored, the poet's treatment of each theme and so forth.

p.81 *The Lady's-Maid's Song*

- Is this poem just fun, or is it making a serious (feminist) point? Does it have to be either one or the other?

- Explain what the poet means by 'he'll have her heart' (line 20). Is this the 'interest' referred to in the last line?

p.81 *Departure Lounge*

- 'Each time we die a little' (lines 9–10). Do you agree with the implication that these extreme feelings are experienced only by the young? Discuss, for example, whether the persona no longer feels 'devastated' at partings.

- How do you interpret the last three lines of the poem?

p.82 *Koriabo*

Title: 'Koriabo' – tributary of the Barima river in the North-West district of Guyana.

- Who is the persona of this poem speaking to, and why?

- Describe in your own words the qualities of the 'love' that the poet longs for in lines 13–15.

p.83 *Sonnet 73*

- Notice the way Shakespeare uses three different metaphors to express the same idea – one in each of the three quatrains (groups of 4 lines) of the sonnet. What is the idea being expressed?

- In Shakespeare's sonnets the couplet (the last two lines) is called 'the whip' because it 'lashes back' or comments on the first twelve lines of the poem. How does the couplet in this sonnet comment on the rest of the poem?

p.83 ## Lullaby

This poem attempts perhaps to bridge the gap between the values we traditionally assign to body and soul: i.e. the physical pleasures of the body (often associated with sin) and the spiritual virtues of the soul.

- The 'fashionable madmen' with their 'pedantic, boring cry' about paying the cost (lines 24–26) are the guardians of moral standards of the society. Why is the persona targeting them?
- Time and mortality are strong arguments in the poem against facile moral judgements. Point out two examples of this.

p.85 ## Hate

- The poet suggests that there are two personalities in this poem. Can you explain the differences in the references to 'me' and 'myself' in the poem?
- Which seems to be the genuine self? Does that self experience the 'hate' that is expressed in the poem? If not, what does that self experience?
- Explain the meaning of 'Then myself forced its way through' (line 8).

p.85 ## It is the Constant Image of your Face

- Can you explain the nature of the conflict experienced by the persona in this poem?
- For whom is love expressed by the persona of the poem?
- What is the treachery referred to in line 6?
- What is the nature of the 'treason' the persona has committed? Do you agree with the view that it is treason?
- The persona's two loves possess, in his view, a similar quality. What is that quality?
- In your own words, explain the meaning of lines 16–18.

p.86 ## Light Love

- The poet compares two kinds of love in this poem. What are they? What are the main differences between them?
- Do you agree with the poet's opinion of 'light love'? Does that opinion justify the second way of loving that is described in stanza 3?

p.86 *Silver Wedding*

'fag-ends' (line 3) – cigarette butts.

- What is the significance of the title of the poem?
- What can you infer about the persona's relationship with his children from what is said in lines 9–12?
- What can you infer about the nature of the persona's relationship with his wife from what is said in lines 13–25?
- What can be inferred about the persona's feelings about his marriage? How do you interpret lines 26–28?

RELIGION

Oars

I am an Indian woman
with long hair,
a band of beads
across my forehead.

5   I paddle against desire's deep
slow-dark river,
sliding softly along
in love's canoe.

My words, slender oars,
10 bear my boat forward –
a keel of silk
upon the water.

My fists clenched
round these wooden
15 spears – I row
consistently.

Ahead –
the river grows
Churlish. Rapids
20 Threaten.

My bark of reeds
is frail, light stems –
insufficient.

The current is fierce.
25 A weariness seeps
Into my marrow.

when that time
comes, love,
will you rescue me?

Mahadai Das

p.98

God's Grandeur

The world is charged with the grandeur of God.
    It will flame out, like shining from shook foil;
    It gathers to a greatness, like the ooze of oil
Crushed. Why do men then now not reck his rod?
5 Generations have trod, have trod, have trod;
    And all is seared with trade; bleared, smeared with toil;
    And wears man's smudge and shares man's smell: the soil
Is bare now, nor can foot feel, being shod.

And for all this, nature is never spent;
10   There lives the dearest freshness deep down things;
And though the last lights off the black West went
    Oh, morning, at the brown brink eastward, springs –
Because the Holy Ghost over the bent
    World broods with warm breast and with ah! bright wings.

p.98 *Gerard Manley Hopkins*

Love [3]

Love bade me welcome; yet my soul drew back,
    Guilty of dust and sin.
But quick-eyed Love, observing me grow slack
    From my first entrance in,
5 Drew nearer to me, sweetly questioning
    If I lacked anything.

'A guest,' I answered, 'worthy to be here.'
    Love said, 'You shall be he.'
'I, the unkind, ungrateful? Ah my dear,
10   I cannot look on Thee.'
Love took my hand, and smiling, did reply,
    'Who made the eyes but I?'

'Truth, Lord, but I have marred them; let my shame
    Go where it doth deserve.'

15 'And know you not,' says Love, 'who bore the blame?'
    'My dear, then I will serve.'
'You must sit down,' says Love, 'and taste my meat.'
    So I did sit and eat.

p.98 *George Herbert*

Parasite

That tree has died.
Its topmost branches reach starkly heavenward
In seeming terror or mute supplication
To be rid of this vine that has clung
5 And drained it of existence.
Now its tendrils drape
The lifeless limbs to give itself
As gift in death a shroud
To the thing that gave it life.

10 How careless are the adornments of death.
Such irony
That in sustaining its own life
This vine has drained the very life it thrived upon.
It must be in all nature
15 To desire a death-in-life existence –
As we, shrouded in the foliage of passion,
Seek evanescent joy that
Must only end in death.

But there's this vine
20 Affixed upon a tree
That in death gave its life
To sundry branches.
It must forever be our
Hope in life and
25 Life in death.

p.98 *Hazel Simmons-McDonald*

El Greco: *Espolio*

The carpenter is intent on the pressure of his hand

on the awl   and the trick of pinpointing his strength
through the awl to the wood   which is tough
He has no effort to spare for despoilings
5   or to worry if he'll be cut in on the dice
His skill is vital to the scene   and the safety of the state
Anyone can perform the indignities   It's his hard arms
and craft that hold the eyes of the convict's women
There is the problem of getting the holes exact
10   (in the middle of this elbowing crowd)
and deep enough to hold the spikes
after they've sunk through those bared feet
and inadequate wrists he knows are waiting behind him

He doesn't sense perhaps that one of the hands
15   is held in a curious gesture over him –
giving   or asking   forgiveness? –
but he'd scarcely take time to be puzzled by poses
Criminals come in all sorts   as anyone knows who makes crosses
are as mad or sane as those who decide on their killings
20   Our one at least has been quiet so far
though they say he talked himself into this trouble
a carpenter's son who got notions of preaching

Well here's a carpenter's son who'll have carpenter sons
God willing   and build what's wanted   temples or tables
25   mangers or crosses   and shape them decently
working alone in that firm and profound abstraction
which blots out the bawling of rag-snatchers
To construct with hands   knee-weight   braced thigh
keeps the back turned from death

30   But it's too late now for the other carpenter's boy
to return to this peace before the nails are hammered

p.99   *Earle Birney*

Jesus is Nailed to the Cross

NAOMI   Well in a way it had
To come to dis. Is so
Life stay. If him was just
Anadda likl madman
5   Passing through, dem wouldn'
Haffe kill him. Him mussi
Really God fi true, else
Him would dead t'ree time
A'ready. And now dem
10 Going to lick some royal
Nail into him wrist
And kill him one more time
Before him dead. Look
Samuel. De man whole
15 Body jump each time dem
Bring de hammer down. Blood
Running from him two hand
Like two river. Is lift
Dem Lifting up de cross
20 Now – Samuel, dem nail
So big him weight going tear
Him off it when dem drop
De cross inna de hole.

SAMUEL   Naomi yuh know is
25 Now I see de ting. Dis
Crucifixion is a
Sacrifice. Dis Golgotha,
Hill of de Skull, come like
De altar for de sacrifice.
30 And de man Jesus is de
Offering. And if him
Is God son fi true den
Any how dem kill him, some
Dread dread things going come
35 Upon dis land. So me
Nah leave yah till him dead,
No matta how it bruk
Up mi old body and

Tear mi soul apart. Mi
40 Time well short. Today me
Must find out which priest is
Really priest. Me haffe know
Who have de truth, who have
De power, who me must
45 Follow – de Pharisee dem
or de Nazarene.

p.100 *Pamela Mordecai*

A Stone's Throw

We shouted out
'We've got her! Here she is!
It's her all right'.
We caught her.
5 There she was –

A decent-looking woman, you'd have said,
(They often are)
Beautiful, but dead scared,
Tousled – we roughed her up
10 A little, nothing much

And not the first time
By any means
She'd felt men's hands
Greedy over her body –
15 But ours were virtuous,
Of course.

And if our fingers bruised
Her shuddering skin,
These were love-bites, compared
20 To the hail of kisses of stone,
The last assault
And battery, frigid rape,
To come
Of right.

25   For justice must be done
        Specially when
        It tastes so good.

        And then – this guru,
        Preacher, God-merchant, God-knows-what –
30   Spoilt the whole thing,
        Speaking to her
        (Should never speak to them)
        Squatting on the ground – her level,
        Writing in the dust
35   Something we couldn't read.
        And saw in her
        Something we couldn't see,
        At least until
        He turned his eyes on us,
40   Her eyes on us,
        Our eyes upon ourselves.

        We walked away
        Still holding stones
        That we may throw
45   Another day
        Given the urge.

p.100   ***Elma Mitchell***

Notes and questions

The poems in this section do not deal with religion in a strictly conventional sense. Many of them explore religious customs or beliefs as well as biblical events. Some have references to God/gods but they are not preoccupied solely with religious fervour. You may wish to try writing a summary statement about the theme(s) of each poem.

p.91 *Oars*

- The poem is an extended metaphor about paddling a canoe against the tide of a river. What do you think the poet is really talking about?
- In which stanza does the poet begin to think about the future? Quote lines or phrases that show that her confidence has begun to falter.
- What solution does she see to her problems?

p.92 *God's Grandeur*

- Pay some attention to the poet's use of rhyme in this poem. Can you detect a distinct pattern?
- Point out a few examples of alliteration in the poem and discuss how they contribute to the tone, colour and meaning of the poem.
- What, do you think, is the effect of the repetition of 'have trod' (line 5)?
- To what does the poet attribute the renewal of nature? How does he view man's role in nature?

p.92 *Love [3]*

- Who is the 'love' referred to in this poem?
- Explain in your own words the situation being described in the poem, and why the persona's soul 'drew back'.
- Which of the following terms best describe the technique of this poem: 'personification', 'allegory', 'metaphor'? Explain your choice.

p.93 *Parasite*

- The poet juxtaposes ideas about life and death in this poem. Try to explain how the vine functions as a symbol of both life and death.

- Do you think that 'this vine' in line 4 is the same as 'this vine' in line 19? To what or to whom does 'this vine' in line 19 refer?

- Think about the references to death. Do you think that 'death' (line 18) and 'death' (line 25) refer to physical and/or spiritual death? Explain your response.

p.94

El Greco: Espolio

Title: 'El Greco' – one of the world's famous painters (1541–1614). He was born in Crete, but did most of his work in Spain. The Spaniards called him El Greco, which means 'the Greek'. It has been said that El Greco distorted form in order to bring the spiritual quality of the subject matter of his work into sharper focus. His paintings are said to embody both the elegance of the court and the fervour of religion.

Espolio – refers to the title of the painting, *El Expolio*, which depicts the disrobing of Christ at the scene of the crucifixion. While Christ is being disrobed a carpenter bends over the cross in the foreground and makes a hole in the cross where one of the nails will go. See the photograph below.

- Several of the references in the poem allude to events surrounding the life of Christ. Discuss how these contribute to the overall meaning of the

El Expolio reproduced with kind permission of Bridgeman Art Library/ Museum of Fine Arts, Budapest

poem. You may begin by discussing some of the following phrases/lines: 'he'll be cut in on the dice' (line 5); 'Our one' (line 20); 'he talked himself into this trouble' (line 21); 'a carpenter's son . . . mangers or crosses' (line 25); 'rag-snatchers' (line 27).

- Discuss the significance of the line 'His skill is vital to the scene and the safety of the state' (line 6).

p.95 ## Jesus is Nailed to the Cross

- What does the use of nation language (dialect) add to this poem?
- Quote four brief passages that indicate that the speakers find it very painful to watch the scene before their eyes.
- State in your own words the decision that Samuel feels he has to make that day (lines 40–46). On what will this decision be based?
- 'Naomi describes what is happening and Samuel tries to understand and interpret it for the reader.' Is this a fair commentary on what the two parts of the poem are doing?

p.96 ## A Stone's Throw

This poem is based on a scene from the New Testament of the Bible in which a woman is about to be stoned. You may read the original account in the Gospel according to John, Chapter 8, Verses 3 to 11.

- Whose is the speaking voice of the poem?
- Can you explain the reference to 'Writing in the dust' (line 34)?
- What do the lines in parentheses (lines 7 and 32) indicate?

CONFLICTS AND COMPLICATIONS

This picture illustrates the poem, 'Green Beret', on page 121 in this section.

Race and Gender

A View of the Caribbean and Its Memories of Our Not-so-Recent Collective Past

To Helen whose gift of a picture of a West Indian harbour made it possible

History-stretched between forgotten ancestors
and cussing new world cousins,
I pause to count our combined sins of blood
and our collective crimes of eternities
5 by the wavelashes that shatter the calm
of the mirror-surface of your sun-framed fortunes
and I contemplate your holiday resorts into
    mosaics of silhouette slave ships
    that sit safe in protected harbours
10   to await the arrival of auctioneers
    and cheap labour merchants,
    shadows that cast shadows
    to map out your white sea breakers
    into the mast-sails that once floated ships
15   which were pregnant with our ancestral limbs,
    luminous dusk-glow that stays the mind
    on the last constants of primordial nightmares
    and details that accentuate details
    to whip our past awake into our present pains.
20 Still, like the sea that now gives you a home and a name,
I wonder if the tidal waves of your brave new world
have whirled you beyond the bedrock of your sea
and washed you past the memorial beacons
of those ancient dreams that predators
25 from within and without our ranks
conspired to discredit and freeze into museum pieces.

p.114   *Funso Aiyejina*

'i will lift up mine eyes . . .'

the rich man, near the summit, looks
through the needle's eye

down on the nouveau riche
blustering up hill, all brass and flash

5   glancing, in the rear-view mirror,
at the middling aspirer behind

who, despite his straight or crooked efforts
won't ever reach the summit

but at least is pleased (thank God)
10 that he is not so far below

as the worker, struggling from a rut
into a blindman's ditch, and cursing at

all unemployed and thieves and beggars
the normal litter spawned in any sty

15 who yet believe that even they
fit in somewhere, therefore are better than

the shocking madman on the dung-heap
who laughs and understands the whole thing.

p.114   *Kendel Hippolyte*

Ultimate

'And the sea gave up the dead . . . and they were judged' (Rev. 20.13)

It is false
the sea will not give up
its honoured dead
the transit slaves
5   who dived into its deep
to rescue drowning freedom.

Their bones are pearls
to gem the crown of Neptune
their bodies make a living
10   sacrament
their spirits light eternal flames
for them there is no judgment.

The sea is sick
to vomit merchantmen
15   who traded chains
those prisoners were martyrs
love-slaves of liberty
they have no case to answer
to die for freedom
20   is the ultimate morality.

p.114   *Howard Fergus*

Test Match Sabina Park

Proudly wearing the rosette of my skin
I strut into Sabina
England boycotting excitement bravely,
something badly amiss.

5   Cricket. Not the game they play at Lords,
the crowd – whoever saw a crowd
at a cricket match? – are caged
vociferous partisans, quick to take offence.

England sixty eight for none at lunch.
10   'What sort o battin dat man?
dem kaaan play cricket again,
praps dem should-a-borrow Lawrence Rowe!'

And on it goes, the wicket slow
as the batting and the crowd restless.
15   'Eh white bwoy, how you brudders dem
does sen we sleep so? Me a pay monies
fe watch dis foolishness? Cho!'

So I try to explain in my Hampshire drawl
about conditions in Kent,
20   about sticky wickets and muggy days
and the monsoon season in Manchester
but fail to convince even myself.

The crowd's loud 'busin drives me out
skulking behind a tarnished rosette
25   somewhat frayed now but unable, quite,
to conceal a blushing nationality.

p.115 **Stewart Brown**

Theme for English B

The instructor said,

> *Go home and write*
> *a page tonight.*
> *And let that page come out of you –*
5   > *Then, it will be true.*

I wonder if it's that simple?
I am twenty-two, colored, born in Winston-Salem.
I went to school there, then Durham, then here
to this college on the hill above Harlem.
10   I am the only colored student in my class.
The steps from the hill lead down into Harlem,
through a park, then I cross St. Nicholas,
Eighth Avenue, Seventh, and I come to the Y,
the Harlem Branch Y, where I take the elevator
15   up to my room, sit down, and write this page:

It's not easy to know what is true for you or me
at twenty-two, my age. But I guess I'm what
I feel and see and hear, Harlem, I hear you:
hear you, hear me – we two – you, me, talk on this page.
20   (I hear New York, too.) Me – who?

Well, I like to eat, sleep, drink, and be in love.
I like to work, read, learn, and understand life.
I like a pipe for a Christmas present,

or records – Bessie, bop, or Bach.
25   I guess being colored doesn't make me *not* like
the same things other folks like who are other races.
So will my page be colored that I write?
Being me, it will not be white.
But it will be
30   a part of you, instructor.
You are white –
yet a part of me, as I am a part of you.
That's American.
Sometimes perhaps you don't want to be a part of me.
35   Nor do I often want to be a part of you.
But we are, that's true!
As I learn from you,
I guess you learn from me –
although you're older – and white –
40   and somewhat more free.

This is my page for English B.

p.115 *Langston Hughes*

Elsa's Version

Lawd God
I tired fe hear it
I tired fe hear it
so till.
5 All dem big talk:
'Women are our natural resources
Women are the backbone
of this country'
Me no bone inna
10 no body back
nor rib outa
no body side.
Is who dem tink
dey a go fool
15 while dem still a
treat we to no-count wages.
An we shouldn' mind

dat we riding fine
in nuff dutty song
20   a boom shaka boom
pon every street corner.

You rass man
stop put we down
in dutty song or
25   high-up editorial.
You can confuse, abuse
an mess wid you own self
till you good an ready
to deal wid I as
30   a real somebody.

Till dat day come

      Lef me alone
      an me modda
      an me sista
35   an me gal-pickney.

p.115   *Christine Craig*

The Tourists

'The sun works for the Tourist Board'
was a bad joke. But now each noon
the sun toils like a fisherman
with a hard tide to beat,
5   or a farmer whose wife will drop soon.

And in truth the beach is replete
with strangers. Each one arranges
tenderly his limbs for those brass rays
as a woman, testing each pose, changes
10   into nothing for her lover's gaze.

The natives mind their own business.
Some blond types are at it again.

An English anthropologist
praises the texture of a seine.
15   The sea's heard it all before.

A scene from a tourist
brochure. Under that sun
all is languid, and those who come
will find nothing unusual, not
20   one gesture or motion overdone.

But for one parrot fish which turns
grave somersaults on the stainless steel
spear that's just usurped its dim
purpose; which was to swim
25   as usual through blue air, in silence, like the sun.

p.116   *Wayne Brown*

[handwritten: 5 stanzas, 1st 3 - 7 lines, last 2 - 5 lines, rhythm scheme - free verse, run on lines]

Dreaming Black Boy

I wish my teacher's eyes wouldn't
go past me today. Wish he'd know
it's okay to hug me when I kick
a goal. Wish I myself wouldn't
5   hold back when an answer comes.
I'm no woodchopper now
like all ancestors.

[handwritten: The boy wants his teacher to notice him. Hug him just because he is black and that he wouldn't be intimidated to answer in class because of his skin colour.]

I wish I could be educated
to the best of tune up, <u>and earn</u>
10   <u>good money</u> and not sink <u>to lick</u>
<u>boots.</u> I wish I could go on every
crisscross way of the globe
and no persons or powers or
hotel keepers would make it a waste.

[handwritten: He wants to learn but is being deprived of it due to his skin colour. He doesn't want to have to suck up or be below the white man but be independent!]

15   I wish life wouldn't spend me out
[handwritten: defending] opposing. Wish same way creation
would have me stand it would have
me stretch, and hold high, my voice
Paul Robeson's, <u>my inside eye</u>

[handwritten: segregation limited, kept away from due to his skin colour]

[handwritten: proud of himself]

20 a sun. Nobody wants to say
hello to nasty answers.

I wish <u>torch throwers of night</u> *[handwritten: white people, white supremacist groups. white people make him feel different and alienated.]*
would burn lights for decent times.
Wish plotters in pyjamas would pray
25 for themselves. Wish people wouldn't
talk as if I dropped from Mars.

[handwritten: boast / tallness] I wish only boys were scared
behind <u>bravados</u>, for I could suffer.
I could suffer a big big lot.
30 I wish nobody would want to earn
the <u>terrible burden I can suffer.</u> *[handwritten: being black - hated, likes, outcast, segregated.]*

p.116 *James Berry*

Infidelities

[handwritten: speaker responds hopeful.]

Two boys battle on a flat, green field,
outside the village. At noon, when my sister
brings them thick, flaked flour-cakes
and her water-cool voice, both will yield.

5 There are no more dragons to fight to the death,
and young hearts are hot as the leaping sun;
that is why, and because she has smiled at one,
they shiver the gay air with their breath.
How jealous they are! How vainly they fight!
10 I watch the dark brown boys and laugh;
my sister is safe; when boys, at night,
in these islands, dream, their dreams are white.

p.116 *Dennis Scott*

The Lynching

[handwritten: speaker - a holy sacrifice. (biased speaker) white people - a demonic "]

His spirit in smoke ascended to high heaven. *[handwritten: christ dead hanged to death]*
His father, by the cruellest way of pain,
Had bidden him to his bosom once again; *[handwritten: father reflecting to god.]*

The awful sin remained <u>still unforgiven.</u>
5 All night a bright and solitary star
(Perchance the one that ever guided him,
Yet gave him up at last to Fate's wild whim)
Hung pitifully o'er the swinging char.
Day dawned, and soon the <u>mixed crowds</u> came to view
10 <u>The ghastly body swaying in the sun:</u>
The women thronged to look, but never a one
Showed sorrow in <u>her eyes of steely blue;</u>
<u>And little lads, lynchers that were to be,</u>
<u>Danced round the dreadful thing in fiendish glee.</u> — *devil*
little white boys

Handwritten margin note: Description of white people

p.116   *Claude McKay*

Epitaph

They hanged him on a clement morning, swung
between the falling sunlight and the women's
breathing, like a black apostrophe to pain.
All morning while the children hushed
5 their hopscotch joy and the cane kept growing
he hung there sweet and low.
                At least that's how
they tell it. It was long ago
and what can we recall of a dead slave or two
10 except that when we punctuate our island tale
they swing like sighs across the brutal
sentences, and anger pauses
till they pass away.

p.116   *Dennis Scott*

Caribbean History

A flower falls on a leaf,
the forest sleeps, and
waves are on holiday.

El Dorado sings of love
5 as Columbus listens
in a plastic boat.
Guacanagari flies to New York,
– Nobody needs the Sargasso.
Juliet watches soap operas,
10 and wonders where
real heroes are gone.
Magdalene stops by a store
named, 'Apostles' Feet'.
– What are winged sandals for?
15 Exploring city slums
in a purple limousine
Cleopatra examines
all painted doors.
Other VIPs visit
20 St. Elsewhere-in-the-Sun
for rum and water skis.

There is no oracle,
only fraudulent cinemas.
Elections come –
25 now and then,
like bowls of free soup.
Old Moses says.
– Democracy works!
Citizens of some lands
30 stare in one-eyed belief.

But rum-jumbies
dance with people, and
– who don't see don't care.

p.117

Stanley Greaves

For Rosa Parks

And how was this soft-voiced woman to know
that this 'No'
in answer to the command to rise
would signal the beginning

5   of the time of walking?
Soft the word
like the closing of some aweful book
a too-long story
with no pauses for reason
10   but yes, an ending
and the signal to begin the walking.
But the people had walked before
in yoked formations down to Calabar
into the belly of close-ribbed whales
15   sealed for seasons
and unloaded to walk again
alongside cane stalks tall as men.
No, walking was not new to them.
Saw a woman tie rags to her feet
20   running red, burnishing the pavements,
a man with no forty acres
just a mule
riding towards Jerusalem
And the children small somnambulists
25   moving in the before day morning
And the woman who never raised her voice
never lowered her eyes
just kept walking
leading us towards sunrise.

p.117   *Lorna Goodison*

The Sleeping Zemis

He kept the zemis under his bed for years
after the day he came upon them in a cave
which resembled the head of a great stone god,
the zemis placed like weights at the tip of its tongue.

5   Arawaks had hidden them there when they fled,
or maybe the stone god's head was really a temple.
Now under his bed slept three zemis,
wrought from enduring wood of ebony.

The first was a man god who stood erect, his arms
10　folded below his belly. The second was a bird god
　　in flight. The third was fashioned in the form
　　of a spade, in the handle a face was carved.

　　A planting of the crops zemi,
　　a god for the blessing of the corn,
15　for the digging of the sweet cassava
　　which requires good science

　　to render the white root safe food.
　　And over the fields the john crows wheel
　　and the women wait for the fishermen
20　to return from sea in boats hollowed from trees.

　　Under his bed the zemis slept.
　　Where were they when Columbus
　　and his men, goldfever and quicksilver
　　on the brain, came visiting destruction?

25　Man god we gave them meat, fish and cassava.
　　Silent deity we mended their sails, their leaking
　　ships, their endless needs we filled even with
　　our own lives, our own deaths.

　　Bird god, we flew to the hills,
30　their tin bells tolling the deaths
　　of our children, their mirrors
　　foreshadowing annihilation to follow.

　　Spade god we perished.
　　Our spirits wander wild and restless.
35　There was no one left to dig our graves,
　　no guides to point us the way to Coyaba.

　　He turned them over to the keepers of history,
　　they housed them in glass-sided caves.
　　Then he went home to sleep without the gods
40　who had slumbered under his bed for years.

p.118 *Lorna Goodison*

Notes and questions

This section explores material that describes attitudes to race, gender relationships and, in the case of one or two poems, class issues. Some of the poems are concerned with concepts like exile and slavery and the consequences of these experiences. Others are concerned with the question of self-identification and what it means to live in a multi-racial world in which colour can still be a barrier between peoples.

p.102 *A View of the Caribbean* . . .

'primordial' (line 17) – relating to an earlier time in history, the past.

- The poet seems to be focusing on two worlds: what are they? In formulating your answer try to find phrases that describe these worlds; for example, on the one hand the poet uses 'forgotten ancestors' (line 1), 'combined sins of blood' (line 3), 'collective crimes' (line 4) and so on. On the other hand he uses 'sun-framed fortunes' (line 6), 'holiday resorts' (line 7), 'brave new world' (line 21) and so forth. You may also consider the ways in which the 'brave new world' reminds the poet of the past, and in what ways the poet thinks the two worlds are similar.

- In what ways does the title of the poem focus on the meaning of the poem?

p.103 *'i will lift up mine eyes . . .'*

- The poet seems to be presenting 'success' as a progression of stages. Read the poem carefully and find out what those stages are.

- Would you say that the poet has a sympathetic view of people? If not why not?

- How would you describe the tone of the poem?

p.103 *Ultimate*

- Compare this poem with the poem by Funso Aiyejina on p. 102. Would you say that both poets share similar views about slavery?

- What do the following lines tell you about the poet's opinion of the slaves: 'for them there is no judgement' (line 12), 'They have no case to answer' (line 18).

p.104 *Test Match Sabina Park*

Title: 'Sabina Park' – the home of test cricket in Jamaica.
Lines 3–4 – this is a comment on the English style of batting and the grim situation at the crease; however the poet is also punning on the names of England's opening batsmen at the time: Geoff Boycott and Dennis Amiss. 'Lords' (line 5) – cricket ground in England where test matches are played. Stanzas 3 and 4 contain examples of Jamaican creole: 'kaaan' (line 11) – can't; 'Cho!' (line 17) – an expression of annoyance.

- The poet suggests that spectators at Sabina Park are different from those at Lord's; in what ways are they different?
- Can you tell what the nationality of the poet is? What clues are given in the poem?
- Explain the meaning of the last stanza.

p.105 *Theme for English B*

'Winston-Salem' and 'Durham' (lines 7–8) – towns in North Carolina.

- The 'college' referred to in line 9 is in New York City as are the streets, places and buildings mentioned in lines 12–14. What do these specific geographical references contribute to the poem?
- Line 24. The references show the persona's wide tastes in music: 'Bessie' refers to Bessie Smith, an American Blues singer; bop, to a kind of jazz; Bach to the European Classical composer.
- Why do you think the persona mentions the white instructor towards the end of the poem?

p.106 *Elsa's Version*

- The poet is protesting several different things; what are they?
- This poem is also in Jamaican creole. Do you think the same effect would be achieved if the poem were written in Standard English? Why or why not?
- What, in your opinion, is the statement about women the poet is making?
- Are you sympathetic with the poet's point of view? What are your own views on the subject? Try expressing them in poetic form using either dialect or Standard English.

p.107 *The Tourists*

'seine' (line 14) – a fishing net.

- What is indicated by the line 'the sea's heard it all before' (line 15)?

- The sun is a controlling image in the poem. Find the various references to the sun and explain how these references contribute to your understanding of the meaning of the poem.

- What are the main comments that the poet is making about tourism? How would you describe his attitude to it?

- What is your opinion of tourism? Is it similar to the opinion of the poet?

p.108 *Dreaming Black Boy*

'torch throwers of night' (line 22) – possibly a specific reference to the Ku Klux Klan but generally to all destructive groups that engage in such actions.

- In expressing his wishes for different things, the persona of the poem is at the same time lamenting certain attitudes or behaviours. For each wish or set of wishes in each stanza, find one or two words, other than those used in the poem, which describe exactly what the boy is longing for.

- How does the last stanza contribute to the overall meaning of the poem? Do you think that the burden referred to in the last stanza has been explained in the rest of the poem?

p.109 *Infidelities*

- What is the poet describing? Summarise in two or three lines what the poem is about.

- What is meant by 'There are no more dragons . . . sun' (lines 6–7)? Think about the practice of fighting dragons in the past, and why knights in armour reportedly did so.

- Why does the poet think his sister is safe?

- Do you agree with the view expressed in the last line of the poem?

p.109 –110 *The Lynching* and *Epitaph*

- Both McKay and Scott write about a lynching and capture the horror of such an incident in different ways. How?

- What do the poets focus on?

- Where is the turning point in McKay's poem?

- Both poets describe the onlookers' reactions to the scenes. What would you say are the differences in these reactions?

- Scott goes beyond description to make a comment (lines 9–13). Discuss the meaning and the purpose of that comment.

p.110

Caribbean History

'El Dorado' (line 4) – the fabled golden city in South America sought and written about by the Spanish Conquistadors and other adventurers like Walter Raleigh.

'Sargasso' (line 8) – a stagnant area of the Atlantic ocean, caught between area currents and supposedly covered with weeds and other marine growths. It might also be a reference to Jean Rhys's novel *Wide Sargasso Sea*. The other references are to various icons of Western history and contemporary popular culture.

- Is the persona merely showing off, with all of these allusions, or do they tell us something about the Caribbean and its history?
- What figure of speech is found in the middle of the third stanza (line 26) and what does it tell us about the persona's attitude towards Caribbean politics?
- What does the last stanza mean?

p.111

For Rosa Parks

Title: 'Rosa Parks' – a black woman who in 1955 refused to give up her seat to a white passenger on a bus in Montgomery, Alabama. As a result of her refusal, Parks was arrested and other blacks staged a boycott of the Montgomery bus system in protest. The boycott lasted for a year and the incident initiated the Civil Rights movement in the United States of America.

'Calabar' (line 13) – a river and the surrounding region in Nigeria.

'close-ribbed whales' (line 14) – not literal whales but a reference to slave ships.

- According to Goodison's account how significant is the form of protest that was used?
- To what events in history do the following lines refer? 'But the people had walked . . .' (lines 12–17); 'a man with no forty acres . . . Jerusalem' (lines 21–23).
- Can you tell what parallels Goodison is attempting to draw between these events and the Rosa Parks incident?
- Discuss the importance of the final line to an understanding of the events described in the poem.

- Find more information about the Rosa Parks incident and its significance in changing the course of history in the United States.
- Re-read the poem and discuss the ways in which the 'word' (line 6) was 'an ending' (line 10) and a beginning (line 11).

p.112 ## The Sleeping Zemis

Zemi – a carved figure of a god in Amerindian culture.

- What is the poet saying about the Amerindian peoples in this poem?
- Explain the significance of the word 'sleeping' in the title, along with the repetition of 'slept' and the word 'slumbered' in the body of the poem.

Dulce et Decorum Est

Bent double, like old beggars under sacks,
Knock-kneed, coughing like hags, we cursed through sludge,
Till on the haunting flares we turned our backs
And towards our distant rest began to trudge.
5   Men marched asleep. Many had lost their boots
But limped on, blood-shod. All went lame; all blind;
Drunk with fatigue; deaf even to the hoots
Of tired, outstripped Five-Nines that dropped behind.

Gas! GAS! Quick, boys! – An ecstasy of fumbling,
10 Fitting the clumsy helmets just in time;
But someone still was yelling out and stumbling,
And flound'ring like a man in fire or lime . . .
Dim, through the misty panes and thick green light,
As under a green sea, I saw him drowning.

15 In all my dreams, before my helpless sight,
He plunges at me, guttering, choking, drowning.

If in some smothering dreams you too could pace
Behind the wagon that we flung him in,
And watch the white eyes writhing in his face,
20 His hanging face, like a devil's sick of sin;
If you could hear, at every jolt, the blood
Come gargling from the froth-corrupted lungs,
Obscene as cancer, bitter as the cud
Of vile, incurable sores on innocent tongues, –
25 My friend, you would not tell with such high zest
To children ardent for some desperate glory,
The old Lie: Dulce et decorum est
Pro patria mori.

p.125   *Wilfred Owen*

Bayonet Charge

Suddenly he awoke and was running – raw
In raw-seamed hot khaki, his sweat heavy,
Stumbling across a field of clods towards a green hedge
That dazzled with rifle fire, hearing
5   Bullets smacking the belly out of the air –
He lugged a rifle numb as a smashed arm:
The patriotic tear that had brimmed in his eye
Sweating like molten iron from the centre of his chest –

In bewilderment then he almost stopped –
10   In what cold clockwork of the stars and the nations
Was he the hand pointing that second? He was running
Like a man who has jumped up in the dark and runs
Listening between his footfalls for the reason
Of his still running, and his foot hung like
15   Statuary in mid-stride. Then the shot-slashed furrows

Threw up a yellow hare that rolled like a flame
And crawled in a threshing circle, its mouth wide
Open silent, its eyes standing out.
He plunged past with his bayonet toward the green hedge.
20   King, honour, human dignity, etcetera
Dropped like luxuries in a yelling alarm
To get out of that blue crackling air
His terror's touchy dynamite.

p.125   *Ted Hughes*

And there is an anger . . .

And there is an anger
In that bronze patience
Tied to the murmur of his fingers.
Those speaking eyes,
5   Squatting on me,
Take up my helplessness
Against his communal gestures.

An apologetic fidget in the chair
Adjusts his harshness.

10   He is is a son of the soil who roves
The outskirts of our jungle;
He is our brother who moves
With the sun so easily.
Still,

15   His eyes have strange fires.
Will there be time,
For us, for me
Groping for a neutral gentleness
To reach him without burning,
20   To lift into laughter?

p.125   *Edwin Thumboo*

Green Beret

He was twelve years old,
and I do not know his name.
The mercenaries took him and his father,
whose name I do not know,
5   one morning upon the High Plateau.
Green Beret looked down on the frail boy
with the eyes of a hurt animal and thought,
a good fright will make him talk.
He commanded, and the father was taken away
10   behind the forest's green wall.
'Right kid tell us where they are,
tell us where or your father – dead.'
With eyes now bright and filled with terror
the slight boy said nothing.

15   'You've got one minute kid', said Green Beret,
'tell us where or we kill father'
and thrust his wrist-watch against a face all eyes,
the second-hand turning, jerking on its way.
'OK boy ten seconds to tell us where they are'

20 In the last instant the silver hand shattered the sky and the forest of trees.
'Kill the old guy' roared Green Beret
and shots hammered out
behind the forest's green wall
and sky and trees and soldiers stood
25 in silence, and the boy cried out.
Green Beret stood
in silence, as the boy crouched down
and shook with tears,
as children do when their father dies.

30 'Christ', said one mercenary to Green Beret
'he didn't know a damn thing
we killed the old guy for nothing'
so they all went away
Green Beret and his mercenaries.

35 And the boy knew everything.
He knew everything about them, the caves,
the trails the hidden places and the names,
and in the moment that he cried out,
in that same instant
40 protected by frail tears
far stronger than any wall of steel
they passed everywhere
like tigers
across the High Plateau.

p.126 *Ho Thien*

Listening to Sirens

Was it the air-raids that I once lived through
listening to sirens, then the bombers' drone
that makes the spring night charter to Corfu
wake me at 2, alarmed, alert, alone?
5 I watch its red light join the clustered stars
in the one bright clearing in the overcast
then plummet to become a braking car's
cornering deserted side-streets far too fast.

My lilac purples as the headlamps pass
10 and waft it in, that same lilac smell
that once was used to sweeten mustard gas
and induce men to inhale the fumes of hell.
A thin man from that War who lived round here
used to go berserk on nights like these,
15 cower, scream, and crap his pants with fear
whenever he scented lilac on the breeze.

Senses that have been blighted in this way
or dulled by dark winter long for the warm South,
some place we hollow out for holiday,
20 and nothing spoils the white wine in the mouth.
I drag my senses back into the dark
and think of those pale Geordies on their flight.
I'll still be oblivious when they disembark
dazzled by the blue and the bright light.

p.126 *Tony Harrison*

This is the dark time, my love

This is the dark time, my love,
All round the land brown beetles crawl about.
The shining sun is hidden in the sky.
Red flowers bend their heads in awful sorrow.

5 This is the dark time, my love.
It is the season of oppression, dark metal, and tears.
It is the festival of guns, the carnival of misery.
Everywhere the faces of men are strained and anxious.

Who comes walking in the dark night time?
10 Whose boot of steel tramps down the slender grass?
It is the man of death, my love, the strange invader
Watching you sleep and aiming at your dream.

p.126 *Martin Carter*

Sonnets from China XV

As evening fell the day's oppression lifted;
Far peaks came into focus; it had rained:
Across wide lawns and cultured flowers drifted
The conversation of the highly trained.

5 Two gardeners watched them pass and priced their shoes;
A chauffeur waited, reading in the drive,
For them to finish their exchange of views;
It seemed a picture of the private life.

Far off, no matter what good they intended,
10 The armies waited for a verbal error
With all the instruments for causing pain:

And on the issue of their charm depended
A land laid waste, with all its young men slain,
Its women weeping, and its towns in terror.

p.126   *W. H. Auden*

124

Notes and questions

The poems in this group deal with the cruelty, the pain and the suffering of war, the weapons, the bravery, the loss (the waste) of life. Notice how in some poems the horrors of war are juxtaposed with images of the beauty and serenity of nature, in order to insist, as it were, that there is an alternative world, at least as large and as real as that of the raging conflict.

p.119 *Dulce et Decorum Est*

Title – From the Latin saying 'Dulce et Decorum Est Pro Patria Mori' 'It is pleasant and befitting to die for one's country'.

- Notice the contrast between the title (explained above) and the poem itself. What is the poet really saying about fighting in wars for one's country?

p.120 *Bayonet Charge*

'clods' (line 3) – lumps of earth or mud.
- What are some of the words in the first stanza that help to suggest the frenzy of the action taking place?
- In stanza 2 the charging soldier almost stops because a sudden thought hits him. What thought?
- Note the hare that has been shot (stanza 3) – an innocent victim of the fighting. Compare this with the juxtaposition of natural images and the memories of the horrors of war in 'Listening to Sirens' by Tony Harrison.
- How is the soldier's situation different from that of the hare?

p.120 *And there is an anger . . .*

- There is no mention of fighting in this poem, yet conflict is implied between the 'son of the soil' (line 10) whose 'eyes have strange fires' (line 15) and the narrator, 'groping for a neutral gentleness' (line 18). Note how words on their own can suggest situations that are not overtly stated.
- Is there anything else in the poem that points to conflict or potential conflict?

p.121 ## Green Beret

This narrative poem tells of an incident during the war in Vietnam.

- What is the effect of the repeated reference to the invading soldier as 'Green Beret'?

- There is an effective contrast between Green Beret's anonymous, brutal exercise of power and the frail, terrified helplessness of the little boy and his father. There are several other such contrasts in the poem; can you point out a few of them? What is the irony shown by such contrasts?

- Whose side is the persona on and how can you tell?

p.122 ## Listening to Sirens

'Geordies' (line 22) – a name for people from the north-east of England (Newcastle/Durham area).

- Is this a poem about war? Compare this with 'Dulce et Decorum Est'.

p.123 ## This is the dark time, my love

This poem is set in British Guiana at the time when the Governor suspended the Constitution and British soldiers were sent in to 'maintain order'.

- This is another poem that juxtaposes guns and soldiers with things of nature ('red flowers' – line 4, 'slender grass' – line 10). Why do you think this juxtaposition is so frequently used in this type of poem?

- What is the effect of the repeated reference to 'my love' in the poem?

- In the last line the 'man of death' is 'aiming at your dream'. What does this mean? What is threatened by the soldiers if not life itself?

p.124 ## Sonnets from China XV

This poem is a sonnet. The first eight lines are called the 'octave' and the last six the 'sestet', and the division is frequently used to emphasise a contrast or a change in mood or perspective. In this poem the contrast is between the peace, order and luxury of the embassy lawns and the confusion, suffering and death that will be inflicted by the armies waiting for the signal.

THE STRANGE AND THE SUPERNATURAL

My Mother's Sea Chanty

I dream that I am washing
my mother's body in the night sea
and that she sings slow
and that she still breathes.

5   I see my sweet mother
a plump mermaid in my dreams
and I wash her white hair
with ambergris and foaming seaweed.

I watch my mother under water
10   gather the loose pearls she finds,
scrub them free from nacre
and string them on a lost fishing line.

I hear my dark mother
speaking sea-speak with pilot fish,
15   showing them how to direct barks
that bear away our grief and anguish.

I pray my mother breaks free
from the fish pots and marine chores
of her residence beneath the sea,
20   and that she rides a wild white horse.

p.133 *Lorna Goodison*

Mirror

I am silver and exact. I have no preconceptions.
Whatever I see I swallow immediately
Just as it is, unmisted by love or dislike.
I am not cruel, only truthful –

5   The eye of a little god, four-cornered.
Most of the time I meditate on the opposite wall.
It is pink, with speckles. I have looked at it so long
I think it is part of my heart. But it flickers.
Faces and darkness separate us over and over.

10   Now I am a lake. A woman bends over me,
Searching my reaches for what she really is.
Then she turns to those liars, the candles or the moon.
I see her back, and reflect it faithfully.
She rewards me with tears and an agitation of hands.
15   I am important to her. She comes and goes.
Each morning it is her face that replaces the darkness.
In me she has drowned a young girl, and in me an old woman
Rises toward her day after day, like a terrible fish.

p.133 *Sylvia Plath*

Ol' Higue

You think I like this stupidness –
gallivanting all night without skin,
burning myself out like cane-fire
to frighten the foolish?
5   And for what? A few drops of baby blood?
You think I wouldn't rather
take my blood seasoned in fat
black-pudding, like everyone else?
And don't even talk 'bout the pain of salt
10   and having to bend these old bones down
to count a thousand grains of rice!

If only babies didn't smell so nice!
And if I could only stop
hearing the soft, soft call
15   of that pure blood running in new veins,
singing the sweet song of life
tempting an old, dry-up woman who been
holding her final note for years and years,
afraid of the dying hum . . .

20   Then again, if I didn't fly and come
      to that fresh pulse in the middle of the night,
      how would you, mother,
      name your ancient dread?
      And who to blame
25   for the murder inside your head . . .?
      Believe me –
      As long as it have women giving birth
      a poor ol' higue like me can never dead.

p.133   *Mark McWatt*

The Daemon-Brother

With growing darkness threatening
to overwhelm my light,
I cried for help.   My brother
tittered at my plight;

5   and while I did my level best
to keep the candle lit
he cheerfully reviewed
the guttering of my wit.

Astonished that the brother found
10   my struggle such a treat
I turned the flickering light on him
and glimpsed his cloven feet.

p.134   *Mervyn Morris*

The Listeners

'Is there anybody there?' said the Traveller,
   Knocking on the moonlit door;
And his horse in the silence champed the grasses
   Of the forest's ferny floor:
5   And a bird flew up out of the turret,

Above the Traveller's head:
And he smote upon the door again a second time;
   'Is there anybody there?' he said.
But no one descended to the Traveller;
10   No head from the leaf-fringed sill
Leaned over and looked into his grey eyes,
   Were he stood perplexed and still.
But only a host of phantom listeners
   That dwelt in the lone house then
15 Stood listening in the quiet of the moonlight
   To that voice from the world of men:
Stood thronging the faint moonbeams on the dark stair,
   That goes down to the empty hall,
Hearkening in an air stirred and shaken
20   By the lonely Traveller's call.
And he felt in his heart their strangeness,
   Their stillness answering his cry,
While his horse moved, cropping the dark turf,
   'Neath the starred and leafy sky;
25 For he suddenly smote on the door, even
   Louder, and lifted his head:–
'Tell them I came, and no one answered,
   That I kept my word', he said.
Never the least stir made the listeners,
30 Though every word he spake
Fell echoing through the shadowiness of the still house
   From the one man left awake:
Ay, they heard his foot upon the stirrup,
   And the sound of iron on stone,
35 And how the silence surged softly backward,
   When the plunging hoofs were gone.

p.134   *Walter De La Mare*

'Le loupgarou'

A curious tale that threaded through the town
Through greying women sewing under eaves,
Was how his greed had brought old Le Brun down,
Greeted by slowly shutting jalousies

5   When he approached them in white-linen suit,
Pink glasses, cork hat, and tap-tapping cane,
A dying man licensed to sell sick fruit,
Ruined by fiends with whom he'd made a bargain.
It seems one night, these Christian witches said,
10   He changed himself to an Alsatian hound,
A slavering lycanthrope hot on a scent,
But his own watchman dealt the thing a wound
Which howled and lugged its entrails, trailing wet
With blood back to its doorstep, almost dead.

p.134   *Derek Walcott*

La Belle Dame Sans Merci

(First version)

O what can ail thee, Knight at arms,
    Alone and palely loitering?
The sedge has withered from the Lake
    And no birds sing!

5   O what can ail thee, Knight at arms,
    So haggard, and so woe begone?
The Squirrel's granary is full
    And the harvest's done.

I see a lily on thy brow
10   With anguish moist and fever dew,
And on thy cheeks a fading rose
    Fast withereth too –

I met a Lady in the Meads,
    Full beautiful, a faery's child
15   Her hair was long, her foot was light
    And her eyes were wild –

I made a Garland for her head,
    And bracelets too, and fragrant Zone
She look'd at me as she did love
20   And made sweet moan –

I set her on my pacing steed
And nothing else saw all day long
For sidelong would she bend and sing
A faery's song –

25 She found me roots of relish sweet
And honey wild and manna dew
And sure in language strange she said
I love thee true –

She took me to her elfin grot
30 And there she wept and sigh'd full sore,
And there I shut her wild wild eyes
With kisses four.

And there she lulled me asleep
And there I dream'd, Ah Woe betide!
35 The latest dream I ever dreamt
On the cold hill side.

I saw pale Kings, and Princes too
Pale warriors, death pale were they all;
They cried, La belle dame sans merci
40 Thee hath in thrall.

I saw their starv'd lips in the gloam
With horrid warning gaped wide,
And I awoke, and found me here
On the cold hill's side.

45 And this is why I sojourn here
Alone and palely loitering;
Though the sedge is withered from the Lake
And no birds sing –

p.134   *John Keats*

Notes and questions

The poems in this group range from those that suggest a strange or puzzling event or situation to those that deal with the creatures of folk superstitions, like the Ol' Higue and the Werewolf, to those that focus on the supernatural and the macabre, like the ghosts in 'The Listeners'. Compare the people and events you encounter in these poems with those in tales you have heard along similar lines. Try to decide what it is we find attractive about such themes.

p.127 *My Mother's Sea Chanty*

'ambergris' (line 8) – a wax-like substance, the colour of ash, found floating in tropical seas. It is used in making perfumes.

'nacre' (line 11) – sometimes called 'mother-of-pearl'. It is a smooth, shining iridescent substance forming the lining of many sea shells.

- The poem's diction clearly indicates an undersea world. Why does the persona picture her mother in such a world?

- If the persona's mother is dead, how would you interpret the wish for her to 'break free' (line 17) and to ride a wild white horse (line 20)?

p.127 *Mirror*

Here the mirror is addressing you, the reader, describing its role in the lives of people.

- How does the poem make us uneasy about the mirror and its role?

- Why does the mirror call itself 'a little god' (line 5)?

- Why is the mirror 'important' (line 15) to the woman in stanza 2?

- The last two lines of the poem are not to be taken literally. What do they mean?

p.128 *Ol' Higue*

A version of the vampire, the Ol' Higue (called a soucouyant in Trinidad and some other islands) is an old woman who sheds her skin at night, transforms herself into a ball of fire and flies about looking for human victims in order to suck their blood. In some traditions her victims are always babies or very young children.

- The Ol' Higue in this poem is obviously not happy with what she does; tell in your own words why she continues to do it.
- What does the final stanza say about our need to believe in such supernatural beings as the Ol' Higue?

p.129 *The Daemon-Brother*

'tittered' (line 4) – laughed.

- The poet is using light and darkness (and the brother's differing reactions to these) to indicate moral or, perhaps, spiritual values. How would you explain this further?
- What does 'cloven feet' (line 12) indicate?

p.129 *The Listeners*

- How would you describe the atmosphere of this poem?
- Who is the persona addressing when he speaks in lines 27–28 'Tell them I came . . . kept my word . . .'?

p.130 *'Le loupgarou'*

Title: French for 'the werewolf' – a man who can change himself into a wolf, usually under the influence of the full moon.
'Alsatian hound' (line 10) – a German shepherd dog, somewhat similar in appearance to a wolf.
'lycanthrope' (line 11) – another word for werewolf.

- The persona claims to be relating a story told him by 'greying women' (line 2). Why do you think he later refers to these women as 'Christian witches' (line 9)?

p.131 *La Belle Dame Sans Merci*

Translation of title – 'The Beautiful Lady without Pity'.
Note that the first two stanzas set the scene and urge the knight to tell his story. The rest of the poem is the knight's story in his own words.

- The form of this poem is that of a ballad: note the hallmarks of ballad metre – alternating four- and three-stress lines and a rhyme scheme of abcb. Find out as much as you can about the ballad form and see how much of what you learn is found in this poem.
- Explain in your own words what happened to the knight.

FROM TIME TO ETERNITY

This picture illustrates the poem, 'Visions of Us', on page 149 of this section.

ART, ARTIST, ARTEFACT

Photos

The dull red glow
makes liquids
in the shallow pans
seem even more innocent
5   empty paper
the machine's glowing eye

so –
insert the grey transparency
direct it on the paper's blank regard
10   eyes keen in concentration
fingers moving, shaping
sculpting light and shade
the artist's terrible power
to make of what he sees
15   what he wants to be seen
then pass the paper still unmarked
from liquid into liquid
and watch the brutal chemicals
force the reluctant image
20   out of hiding
fashioned not in accordance with its truth
but subject to the power
of those stern hands.

p.143 *Cynthia Wilson*

Stillborn

These poems do not live: it's a sad diagnosis.
They grew their toes and fingers well enough,
Their little foreheads bulged with concentration.
If they missed out on walking about like people
5   It wasn't for any lack of mother love.

O I cannot understand what happened to them!
They are proper in shape and number and every part.
They sit so nicely in the pickling fluid!
They smile and smile and smile and smile at me.
10   And still the lungs won't fill and the heart won't start.

They are not pigs, they are not even fish,
Though they have a piggy and a fishy air –
It would be better if they were alive, and that's what they were.
But they are dead, and their mother near dead with distraction,
15   And they stupidly stare, and do not speak of her.

p.143   *Sylvia Plath*

Sad Steps

Groping back to bed after a piss
I part thick curtains, and am startled by
The rapid clouds, the moon's cleanliness.

Four o'clock: wedge-shadowed gardens lie
5   Under a cavernous, a wind-picked sky.
There's something laughable about this,

The way the moon dashes through clouds that blow
Loosely as cannon-smoke to stand apart
(Stone-coloured light sharpening the roofs below)

10   High and preposterous and separate—
Lozenge of love! Medallion of art!
O wolves of memory! Immensements! No,

One shivers slightly, looking up there.
The hardness and the brightness and the plain
15   Far-reaching singleness of that wide stare

Is a reminder of the strength and pain
Of being young; that it can't come again,
But is for others undiminished somewhere.

p.143   *Philip Larkin*

Why I Am Not a Painter

I am not a painter, I am a poet.
Why? I think I would rather be
a painter, but I am not. Well,

for instance, Mike Goldberg
5   is starting a painting. I drop in.
'Sit down and have a drink' he
says. I drink; we drink. I look
up. 'You have SARDINES in it.'
'Yes, it needed something there.'
10   'Oh.' I go and the days go by
and I drop in again. The painting
is going on, and I go, and the days
go by. I drop in. The painting is
finished. 'Where's SARDINES?'
15   All that's left is just
letters, 'It was too much,' Mike says.

But me? One day I am thinking of
a color: orange. I write a line
about orange. Pretty soon it is a
20   whole page of words, not lines.
Then another page. There should be
so much more, not of orange, of
words, of how terrible orange is
and life. Days go by. It is even in
25   prose, I am a real poet. My poem
is finished and I haven't mentioned
orange yet. It's twelve poems, I call
it ORANGES. And one day in a gallery
I see Mike's painting, called SARDINES.

p.144 *Frank O'Hara*

138

Landscape Painter, Jamaica

for Albert Huie

I watch him set up easel,
Both straddling precariously
A corner of the twisted, climbing
Mountain track.

5   A tireless humming-bird, his brush
Dips, darts, hovers now here, now there,
Where puddles of pigment
Bloom in the palette's wild small garden.

The mountains pose for him
10 In a family group –
Dignified, self-conscious, against the wide blue screen
Of morning; low green foot-hills
Sprawl like grandchildren about the knees
Of seated elders. And behind them, aloof,
15 Shouldering the sky, patriarchal in serenity,
Blue Mountain Peak bulks.

And the professional gaze
Studies positions, impatiently waiting
For the perfect moment to fix
20 Their preparedness, to confine them
For the pleasant formality
Of the family album.

His brush a humming-bird
Meticulously poised . . .
25 The little hills fidgeting,
Changelessly changing,
Artlessly frustrating
The painter's art.

p.144   **Vivian Virtue**

139

Ethics

In ethics class so many years ago
our teacher asked this question every fall:
if there were a fire in a museum
which would you save, a Rembrandt painting
5   or an old woman who hadn't many
years left anyhow? Restless on hard chairs
caring little for pictures or old age
we'd opt one year for life, the next for art
and always half-heartedly. Sometimes
10 the woman borrowed my grandmother's face
leaving her usual kitch to wander
some drafty, half-imagined museum.
One year, feeling clever, I replied
why not let the woman decide herself?
15 Linda, the teacher would report, eschews
the burdens of responsibility.
This fall in a real museum I stand
before a real Rembrandt, old woman,
or nearly so, myself. The colors
20 within this frame are darker than autumn,
darker even than winter – the browns of earth,
though earth's most radiant elements burn
through the canvas. I know now that woman
and painting and season are almost one
25 and all beyond saving by children.

p.144   *Linda Pastan*

A Letter from Brooklyn

An old lady writes me in a spidery style,
Each character trembling, and I see a veined hand
Pellucid as paper, travelling on a skein
Of such frail thoughts its thread is often broken;
5 Or else the filament from which a phrase is hung
Dims to my sense, but caught, it shines like steel,
As touch a line, and the whole web will feel.

She describes my father, yet I forget her face
More easily than my father's yearly dying;
10 Of her I remember small, buttoned boots and the place
She kept in our wooden church on those Sundays
Whenever her strength allowed;
Grey haired, thin voice, perpetually bowed.

'I am Mable Rawlins,' she writes, 'and know both your parents;'
15 He is dead, Miss Rawlins, but God bless your tense:
'Your father was a dutiful, honest,
Faithful and useful person.'
For such plain praise what fame is recompense?
'A horn-painter, he painted delicately on horn,
20 He used to sit around the table and paint pictures.'
The peace of God needs nothing to adorn
It, nor glory nor ambition.
'He is twenty-eight years,' she writes, 'he was called home,
And is, I am sure, doing greater work.'

25 The strength of one frail hand in a dim room
Somewhere in Brooklyn, patient and assured,
Restores my sacred duty to the Word.
'Home, home,' she can write, with such short time to live,
Alone as she spins the blessings of her years;
30 Not withered of beauty if she can bring such tears,
Nor withdrawn from the world that breaks its lovers so;
Heaven is to her the place where painters go,
All who bring beauty on frail shell or horn,
There was all made, thence their lux-mundi drawn,
35 Drawn, drawn, till the thread is resilient steel,
Lost though it seems in darkening periods,
And there they return to do work that is God's.

So this old lady writes, and again I believe,
I believe it all, and for no man's death I grieve.

p.144 **Derek Walcott**

Ars Poetica

A poem should be palpable and mute
As a globed fruit,

Dumb
As old medallions to the thumb,

5   Silent as the sleeve-worn stone
Of casement ledges where the moss has grown –

A poem should be wordless
As the flight of birds.

A poem should be motionless in time
10   As the moon climbs,

Leaving, as the moon releases
Twig by twig the nine-entangled trees,

Leaving, as the moon behind the winter leaves,
Memory by memory the mind –

15   A poem should be motionless in time
As the moon climbs.

A poem should be equal to:
Not true.

For all the history of grief
20   An empty doorway and a maple leaf.

For love
The leaning grasses and two lights above the sea –

A poem should not mean
But be.

p.144   *Archibald Macleish*

Notes and questions

These poems explore the meaning, nature and result of art. They focus on several arts: literature, dramatic performance, mechanical craftsmanship, painting. See if you can identify values, approaches and techniques that are common to several areas of art.

p.135 *Photos*

The 'dull red glow' (line 1) comes from the safe-light in the photographer's darkroom, where a stronger light would spoil the photosensitive materials exposed there.

- The rest of the poem describes the process of transferring the negative image (' grey transparency – line 8) onto paper and causing it to emerge and be fixed there by various chemicals. In this context, can you suggest why the poet uses words like 'terrible' (line 13) and 'brutal' (line 18)?

- What comment do the last three lines make about the nature of art?

p.136 *Stillborn*

- This is a poem about writing poems and about the life poems assume. What does the title mean?

- Explain in your own words what you think the persona means when she says the poems are 'dead' (line 14).

- Why is a live fish or pig better than a dead poem?

- Would you say that this poem is included among those the poet considers 'stillborn'? Why?

p.137 *Sad Steps*

The title is probably an allusion to Sir Philip Sidney's *Astrophil and Stella*, Sonnet 31 (1591): 'With how sad steps, O moon, thou climb'st the skies.'

- Suggest a reason why the poet's own steps may be sad after seeing the moon – focus especially on the final stanza.

p.138

Why I Am Not a Painter

Mike Goldberg (line 4) – a New York artist who did silk-screen prints for Frank O'Hara's *Odes* (1960).

- The two longer stanzas are supposedly contrasting the painter and the poet; do you see any significant differences between the two?

p.139

Landscape Painter, Jamaica

- 'palette' (line 8) – the board upon which a painter mixes colours. Why is it compared to a 'wild small garden'?
- Notice the extended metaphor (stanzas 3 and 4) where the landscape of mountains is compared to a family group posing for a portrait. Do you think this is an effective image?
- In what way does the image of the hummingbird at the beginning of the final stanza influence the rest of that stanza?

p.140

Ethics

Tltle: 'Ethics' – the study of questions of right and wrong – moral questions.

- Note that the persona is remembering her childhood up to line 16 and speaks as an adult in the rest of the poem (lines 15–25). What differences in tone and mood do you see in these two sections of the poem?
- What does the poet mean by saying in the last line 'all are beyond saving by children?'

p.140

A Letter from Brooklyn

Note the structure of this poem: two meditative stanzas reflect upon life and art and enclose a central stanza where the persona conducts a kind of dialogue with the words of the letter sent him by the old lady in Brooklyn. This is appropriate because the lady's words are the centre from which the poem radiates outward – in the poet's memory and in his reflections on art. The poem is also about the renewal of the poet's faith in his art.

'lux-mundi' (line 34) – a Latin phrase meaning 'the light of the world'.

p.142

Ars Poetica

'palpable' (line 1) – something that can be felt or touched.

- This poem consists of a list of images comparing a poem to various other things. Look carefully at each image and decide which are the ones you find most meaningful. Is it necessary, do you think, that they all be equally effective?

- Many of the two-line stanzas rhyme. What is the effect of this?
- Does this poem fit the poet's definition of what a poem should be?

Nostalgia

Himself at Last

This lawyer's niceties paid for his pleasures,
Maintained two sons through university,
Indulged his fat wife's need for jewels.

In his free time he grew anthurium lilies;
5   His wife admired them, passers-by begged for them;
All thought him a true artist at his pastime.

Quibbling was an excellent profession
To this dean of small-island mediocrities;
Until one day a swift, sclerotic stroke
10   Wounded his brain. End of the petty sessions.

His wife has left. His sons have hung *their* shingles.
Now he is what he is, by stern compulsion:
A grower of anthuriums.

Speak praise to heaven for this man's handicaps
15   Which have stripped him at last down to himself.

p.151 *Slade Hopkinson*

Saint Lucia's First Communion

At dusk, on the edge of the asphalt's worn-out ribbon,
in white cotton frock, cotton stockings, a black child stands.
First her, then a small field of her. Ah, it's First Communion!
They hold pink ribboned missals in their hands,

5   the stiff plaits pinned with their white satin moths.
The caterpillar's accordion, still pumping out the myth
along twigs of cotton from whose parted mouths
the wafer pods in belief without an 'if'!

So, all across Saint Lucia thousands of innocents
10   were arranged on church steps, facing the sun's lens,

erect as candles between squinting parents,
before darkness came on like their blinded saint's.

But if it were possible to pull up on the verge
of the dimming asphalt, before its headlights lance
15   their eyes, to house each child in my hands,
to lower the window a crack, and delicately urge

the last moth delicately in, I'd let the dark car
enclose their blizzard, and on some black hill,
their pulsing wings undusted, loose them in thousands to stagger
20   heavenward before it came on: the prejudice, the evil!

p.151   *Derek Walcott*

Return

for Kamau Brathwaite

This is the path to new life and to death,
    renaming the earth with familiar sounds,

calling, calling across the green hills
    in three-part harmony, everything jumping,

5   the way the snare springs you back,
    what to do but jump to the pumping sound.

This is the path by the river, now red,
    now reeking of stale bauxite,

the fish are dead, the shrimp are dead,
10   the sea snake dead, the algae dead.

This is the path of new music that calls
    Africa, calls it without knowing,

the pattern of the drums on the skin.
    This is the way the snare makes you jump.

15   My heart beats like a baby's, alert each time
       I embrace dark nights alone.

Here in the stillness, waiting for the crack
       of something, my head pulses in fear.

Then I look for open fields away from predator
20   gunman, a place to wet my body in night dew.

I have returned to plant new grass, new trees,
       and now I know I have returned knowing only

that when death comes, I will be ready,
       for home fires flame in my tender heart, my heart.

p.151   *Kwame Dawes*

South

But today I recapture the islands'
bright beaches: blue mist from the ocean
rolling into the fishermen's houses.
By these shores I was born: sound of the sea
5   came in at my window, life heaved and breathed in me then
with the strength of that turbulent soil.

Since then I have travelled: moved far from the beaches:
sojourned in stoniest cities, walking the lands of the north
in sharp slanting sleet and the hail,
10   crossed countless saltless savannas and come
to this house in the forest where the shadows oppress me
and the only water is rain and the tepid taste of the river.

We who are born of the ocean can never seek solace
in rivers: their flowing runs on like our longing,
15   reproves us our lack of endeavour and purpose,
proves that our striving will founder on that.
We resent them this wisdom, this freedom: passing us
toiling, waiting and watching their cunning declension down to the sea.

But today I would join you, travelling river,
20 borne down the years of your patientest flowing,
past pains that would wreck us, sorrows arrest us,
hatred that washes us up on the flats;
and moving on through the plains that receive us,
processioned in tumult, come to the sea.

25 Bright waves splash up from the rocks to refresh us,
blue sea-shells shift in their wake
and *there* is the thatch of the fishermen's houses, the path
made of pebbles, and look!
Small urchins combing the beaches
30 look up from their traps to salute us:
they remember us just as we left them.

The fisherman, hawking the surf on this side
of the reef, stands up in his boat
and halloos us: a starfish lies in its pool.
35 And gulls, white sails slanted seaward,
fly into the limitless morning before us.

p.151 *Kamau Brathwaite*

Visions of Us

as an old couple
soft in each other's presence,
a living humming with the quality
of those village stores you hardly see now.
5   Bags of sugar with clusters of bees on them,
a smell that is the smell of everything:
onions and flour, saltfish, rice from Guyana,
the light – if i could just describe the light
and how protecting it was when i was a child,
10 how magical an onion bulb could look
on the grained gleaming counter.
Shops like these buzzed with conversation, hefting of boxes,
the thwack of hatches into codfish bristling with salt,
stories continuing from the day before, the deep dizzying
15 smell of women full of man and child, their skin shiny with life,

dark in a golden light just beyond touching.
The shops held all that – comfortably,
like a sack casually holding 100 lb. of potatoes.
There's no word for the subtle grandeur of such places.
20   Always, you miss it, like you miss
the ordinary massive beauty of the diurnal world.
But that quality,
vast richnesses in ordinary things,
is what I see
25   in visions of us, years from now,
as an old couple.

p.152   *Kendel Hippolyte*

Notes and questions

All the poems in this small group express a longing – for understanding or enlightenment, for permanence, for release from time, for the simpler world of the past. We all feel a version of this kind of longing from time to time and these poems speak to that experience.

p.146 ### *Himself at Last*

'quibbling' (line 7) – refers to arguing legal questions in court.
'sclerotic stroke' (line 8) – stroke caused by the hardening or blockage of blood vessels in the brain.
'His sons have hung *their* shingles' (line 11) – means that they have all become qualified professionals and erected signs outside their places of work.

- Why do you think the persona is happy (lines 14–15) that the man can no longer practise law?

p.146 ### *Saint Lucia's First Communion*

'their blinded saint' (line 12) – St Lucy, the patron saint of the island who, according to legend, was blinded during her martyrdom.

- Note the insect imagery in stanza 2 and later in the poem; this is meant to emphasise the frailty and vulnerability of the young children. Why do these qualities strike the persona at this time?
- Describe in your own words what the persona would like to do to all the children (stanzas 4 and 5) and why?

p.147 ### *Return*

Kwame Dawes is a Jamaican poet and the poem is about returning to Jamaica.

- Explain why the persona seems alert and fearful, especially of darkness.
- What is the reason for the persona's return and what is the poem saying about patriotism?

p.148 ### *South*

- The poet, in exile in northern cities, longs for the sea and his island home. Note that the picture painted of his longed-for seashore is the

151

direct opposite of the details of his present landscape (stanza 2). Is either of these pictures entirely accurate, or has the persona selected and exaggerated the details for a reason? For what reason?

- What are the two roles played by the river in the poem?
- Notice that the poem comes full circle as the final stanza returns to the idyllic landscape of childhood described in stanza 1. What does this tell us about the poet's longing?

p.149 *Visions of Us*

- Why is the memory of the village store so precious to the persona?
- Each of the details mentioned seems very ordinary, yet the persona claims that they add up to a 'subtle grandeur' (line 20). Is there a place or institution in your present world for which you would claim a similar richness of life?
- Is nostalgia something that only affects the old? What do you think you will delight to look back on in memory 'years from now'?

DEATH

It Was the Singing

It was the singing, girl, the singing, it was that
that full my throat and blind my eye
with sunlight. Parson preach good, and didn't
give we no long-metre that day
5 and Judge Hackett make us laugh to hear
how from schooldays Gertie was a rebel
and everybody proud how Sharon talk
strong about her mother and hold her tears.
But the singing was sermon and lesson and eulogy
10 and more, and it was only when we raise
'How Great Thou Art' that I really feel
the sadness and the glory, wave after wave.
Daddy Walters draw a bass from somewhere
we never hear him go before, and Maisie
15 lift a descant and nobody ask her,
but it was the gift they bring, it was
what they had to give and greater
than the paper money overflowing the collection
plate. It was then I know we was people
20 together, never mind the bad-minded and the carry-down
and I even find it in my heart to forgive
that ungrateful Agnes for everything she do me
and I sing and the feelings swelling in my chest
till I had to stop and swallow hard.
25 *Then sings my soul, my saviour God to thee,*
How great thou art, how great thou art . . .
and we was girls again together, Gertie
and me by the river, and then the singing
was like a wide water and Gertie laughing
30 and waving to me from the other side.
Girl, I can't too well describe it.
Was like the singing was bigger than all of we
and making us better than we think we could be,
and all I asking you, girl, is when
35 my time come to go, don't worry
make no fuss bout pretty coffin

and no long eulogy, just a quiet place
where gunman and drug addict don't haunt,
and if they sing me home like how they sing Gertie
40   I say thank you Jesus, my soul will sleep in peace.

p.168 *Edward Baugh*

Grampa

Look him. As quiet as a July river –
bed, asleep, an' trim' down like a tree.
Jesus! I never know the Lord could
squeeze so dry. When I was four
5   foot small I used to say
Grampa, how come you t'in so?
an' him tell me, is so I stay
me chile, is so I stay
laughing, an' fine
10   emptying on me –
laughing? It running from him
like a flood, that old molasses
man. Lord, how I never see?
I never know a man could sweet so, cool
15   as rain; same way him laugh,

I cry now. Wash him. Lay him out.

I know the earth going burn
all him limb dem
as smooth as bone,
20   clean as a tree under the river
skin, an' gather us
beside that distant Shore
bright as a river stone.

p.168 *Dennis Scott*

Long Distance

Though my mother was already two years dead
Dad kept her slippers warming by the gas,
put hot water bottles her side of the bed
and still went to renew her transport pass.

5   You couldn't just drop in. You had to phone.
He'd put you off an hour to give him time
to clear away her things and look alone
as though his still raw love were such a crime.

He couldn't risk my blight of disbelief
10   though sure that very soon he'd hear her key
scrape in the rusted lock and end his grief.
He *knew* she'd just popped out to get the tea.

I believe life ends with death, and that is all.
You haven't both gone shopping; just the same,
15   in my new black leather phone book there's your name
and the disconnected number I still call.

p.168   *Tony Harrison*

For Fergus

When Fergus was dying, I had this fantasy
that when some people die, they ought to leave spaces
like holes in the air where they used to be.

Walking around quite normally, we'd stumble on
                  these places
5   and choke and gasp in vacuum till the realisation:
Oh! This is where he was. We need true memories, not
                      just vague traces.

But well before he died, I'd feel a soul-deep irritation
when he would try to drift and they would shake him,
                    trying to wring

a little more life from him. I wanted him to go with
peaceful celebration.

10 I touched his body after they'd roped it in a sheet so
porters could sling
it casually on to a barrow. He was not in it, though we
felt him there
in the room. And walking down a common Castries
street, later, I wanted to sing,

feeling his sudden joyous presence everywhere.
From far beyond his death, amazed, he sent a living
blessing, tingling through the air.

p.168 *Jane King*

Death the Leveller

The glories of our blood and state
    Are shadows, not substantial things;
There is no armour against Fate;
    Death lays his icy hand on kings:
5   Sceptre and Crown
        Must tumble down,
And in the dust be equal made
With the poor crooked scythe and spade.

Some men with swords may reap the field,
10   And plant fresh laurels where they kill:
But their strong nerves at last must yield;
    They tame but one another still:
        Early or late
        They stoop to fate,
15 And must give up their murmuring breath
When they, pale captives, creep to death.

The garlands wither on your brow;
    Then boast no more your mighty deeds!
Upon Death's purple altar now

20   See where the victor-victim bleeds.
          Your heads must come
          To the cold tomb:
Only the actions of the just
Smell sweet and blossom in their dust.

p.169 *James Shirley*

Death Came to See Me in Hot Pink Pants

Last night, I dreamt
that Death came to see me
in hot-pink pants
and matching waistcoat too.
5   He was a beautiful black saga boy.
Forcing open the small door of my wooden cage,
he filled my frame of vision
with a broad white smile,
and as he reached for my throat,
10   the pink sequins on his shoulders
winked at me.

Last night, I dreamt
that Death came to see me in hot-pink pants.
He was a beautiful black saga boy
15   and I hit him with a polished staff
of yellow wood,
and he went down.
But as he reached for me once more,
Laughing, laughing that saga boy laugh,
20   I awoke, holding myself,
unable to breathe.
How beautiful was Death
in hot-pink pants with matching waistcoat too.

p.169 *Heather Royes*

Dirge Without Music

I am not resigned to the shutting away of loving hearts in the hard ground.
So it is, and so it will be, for so it has been, time out of mind:
Into the darkness they go, the wise and the lovely. Crowned
With lilies and with laurel they go; but I am not resigned.

5   Lovers and thinkers, into the earth with you.
Be one with the dull, the indiscriminate dust.
A fragment of what you felt, of what you knew,
A formula, a phrase remains, – but the best is lost.

The answers quick & keen, the honest look, the laughter, the love,
10   They are gone. They have gone to feed the roses. Elegant and curled
Is the blossom. Fragrant is the blossom. I know. But I do not approve.
More precious was the light in your eyes than all the roses in the world.

Down, down, down into the darkness of the grave
Gently they go, the beautiful, the tender, the kind;
15   Quietly they go, the intelligent, the witty, the brave.
I know. But I do not approve. And I am not resigned.

p.169   *Edna St Vincent Millay*

Death, be not proud . . .

Death, be not proud, though some have called thee
Mighty and dreadful, for thou art not so:
For those whom thou think'st thou dost overthrow
Die not, poor Death; nor yet canst thou kill me.
5   From Rest and Sleep, which but thy pictures be,
Much pleasure, then from thee much more must flow;
And soonest our best men with thee do go –
Rest of their bones and souls' delivery!
Thou'rt slave to fate, chance, kings, and desperate men,
10   And dost with poison, war, and sickness dwell;
And poppy or charms can make us sleep as well
And better than thy stroke. Why swell'st thou then?
    One short sleep past, we wake eternally,
    And death shall be no more: Death, thou shalt die!

p.169   *John Donne*

To an Athlete Dying Young

The time you won your town the race
We chaired you through the market place;
Man and boy stood cheering by,
And home we brought you shoulder-high.

5   Today, the road all runners come,
Shoulder-high we bring you home,
And set you at your threshold down,
Townsman of a stiller town.

Smart lad, to slip betimes away
10   From fields where glory does not stay
And early though the laurel grows
It withers quicker than the rose.

Eyes the shady night has shut
Cannot see the record cut,
15   And silence sounds no worse than cheers
After earth has stopped the ears:

Now you will not swell the rout
Of lads that wore their honours out,
Runners whom renown outran
20   And the name died before the man.

So set, before its echoes fade,
The fleet foot on the sill of shade,
And hold to the low lintel up
The still defended challenge cup.

25   And round that early laurelled head
Will flock to gaze the strengthless dead
And find unwithered on its curls
The garland briefer than a girl's.

p.169 *A. E. Housman*

Old Age Gets Up

Stirs its ashes and embers, its burnt sticks

An eye powdered over, half melted and solid again
Ponders
Ideas that collapse
5   At the first touch of attention

The light at the window, so square and so same
So full-strong as ever, the window frame
A scaffold in space, for eyes to lean on

Supporting the body, shaped to its old work
10 Making small movements in gray air
Numbed from the blurred accident
Of having lived, the fatal, real injury
Under the amnesia

Something tries to save itself – searches
15 For defenses – but words evade
Like flies with their own notions

Old age slowly gets dressed
Heavily dosed with death's night
Sits on the bed's edge

20 Pulls its pieces together
Loosely tucks in its shirt

p.170   *Ted Hughes*

Hot Summer Sunday

Especially on hot summer Sundays
my Grandpa liked to rest
supine in the narrow bathtub
soaking in curved cool water
5   sometimes flipping his toes

or, quite child-like,
toying with a pale green soapcake,
but mostly
staying motionless, eyes closed,
10   lips half-smiling,
limbs outstretched.

That hot summer Sunday
when I looked at him
straightly lying, lips parted,
15   silent in the shallow trough,
a foam of white, frothed and lacy,
set as new suds
about his shaven jawbones,
it seemed he might stir,
20   whistle a relaxed sigh,
unclose those eyelids,
ask me to scrub his back.

p.170   *A. L. Hendriks*

Where Death was Kind

Long had I thought
    Of death
And then they told me
You were dead.
5   I had seen him
Sitting in the ante-room
Eager to be summoned,
So when I heard
You had received him
10   I was silent.

I went to see you
Lying in death's embrace.
I was afraid –
I thought the sight
15   Would tear my heart
To pieces,

And my anger would rise
Against death the intruder.

But when I looked
20   Into your lovely face
And saw the sweet peace
That his kiss
Had implanted,
I could not weep,
25   And I could not be angry.

Ah, sweet is death,
And kindly,
To those who suffer
Unbearable agony:
30   Sweet was death's kiss
Upon your lips –
Beloved one
To whom
He gave His Peace.

p.170 *Una Marson*

Because I Could Not Stop for Death

Because I could not stop for Death –
He kindly stopped for me –
The Carriage held but just Ourselves –
And Immortality.

5   We slowly drove – He knew no haste
And I had put away
My labor and my leisure too,
For His Civility –

We passed the School, where Children strove
10   At Recess – in the Ring –
We passed the Fields of Gazing Grain –
We passed the Setting Sun

Or rather – He passed Us –
The Dews drew quivering and chill –
15 For only Gossamer, my Gown –
My Tippet – only Tulle –

We paused before a House that seemed
A Swelling of the Ground –
The Roof was scarcely visible –
20 The Cornice – in the Ground –

Since then – 'tis Centuries – and yet
Feels shorter than the Day
I first surmised the Horses' Heads
Were toward Eternity –

p.170 **Emily Dickinson**

Brother Bone

Not just brothers, we were close:
Death, first son of my mother
and I, we made one.
As eldest brothers will, he'd constantly advise,
5 prod, goad me toward my good.
He was brusque, even mocking, but without guile.
Most people found him hard; in fact,
my close friends called him Bone
(secretly) and told me he was too exact,
10 severe in his perspective, he was cruel.

Perhaps he was, i never noticed.
i followed, hero-worshipped him because
he was calm, wise, deep in the ways
of everything which lived – each leaf, bird, beast
15 or man. He taught me how to see.

There was a clarity, each thing was haloed
when Death, my brother Bone
pointed it out to me.

I never was alone.
20 I loved him, for his cold light that showed
the truth in things.
i miss him now.

p.171   *Kendel Hippolyte*

Ballad of Birmingham

'Mother dear, may I go downtown
instead of out to play,
and march the streets of Birmingham
in a freedom march today?'

5   'No, baby, no, you may not go,
for the dogs are fierce and wild,
and clubs and hoses, guns and jails
ain't good for a little child.'

'But mother, I won't be alone.
10   Other children will go with me,
and march the streets of Birmingham
to make our country free.'

'No baby, no, you may not go,
for I fear those guns will fire.
15   But you may go to church instead,
and sing in the children's choir.'

She has combed and brushed her nightdark hair,
and bathed rose petal sweet,
and drawn white gloves on her small brown hands,
20   and white shoes on her feet.

The mother smiled to know her child
was in the sacred place,
but that smile was the last smile
to come upon her face.

25   For when she heard the explosion,
her eyes grew wet and wild.

She raced through the streets of Birmingham
calling for her child.

She clawed through bits of glass and brick,
30   then lifted out a shoe.
'O, here's the shoe my baby wore,
but, baby, where are you?'

p.171 **Dudley Randall**

St Ann Saturday

Saturday afternoon. So many shades
of black swinging down the road.
Funeral time.
Nice afternoon she get eh!

5   If.

An so many smaddy turn out
like a ole days funeral

Dats right.

Imagine her time come
10   so quick. Well, de Lord giveth
an de Lord taketh away.

Sure ting.

Children walk lightly, plaits
floating with rainbows of ribbons
15   beside auntie's strong hips, uncle's
suit so dark his body is held in tight,
moves only back, front, front, back.
Auntie's hips roll sedately, heave
like waves beside the dancing plaits.

20   You see her big daughter come from
Canada. Me no like how she look

at all. No sir. She look a way.
Me never memba say she so mawga.
Me mind tell me she catching
25   hard time over dere.

Maybe so an maybe not

Imagine six pickney Miss Martha
raise, she one bring dem up
an send dem out into de world.
30   Six pickney she one
an is one degge, degge daughta
come home fe bury her.
Still an all, dem neva come
when she was hearty, no mek sense
35   de come when she direckly dead.

A dat too.

Starapple leaves, doubled toned
bend quiet over the steady walking,
walking for Miss Martha, gone to rest.
40   The path she walked, food to market
children to school, Sunday to Church,
steady walking. In the end, alone
under the starapple leaves a hush
fell over her, silence of age
45   of no names left to call
to table. Of no news from
Delroy or Maisie or Petal
or Lennie or Edith or Steve.

Nice turnout Miss Martha have,
50   An no Granny Bailey dat from Retreat?
Well I neva. Tink seh she dead
long time. Time passing chile
we all moving down de line weself
True word.

p.171 *Christine Craig*

Amerindian

I suppose you'd say with truth
No one here looks all that 'right'.
But they settle themselves down.
He was all wrong from start to finish;
5   He squatted in his bed half the time
Paddling a strange bateau.

All his life he knew forests,
Forests and the great rivers.
Why bring him in town to die?
10   His soul is damned that way.
Tribal over-arching heaven
Replaced by rag of sky.

He should have been with brothers,
He should have died with jaguars and stars
15   And a wind rising in the trees.
A last wood-fire comforting
The coming on of cold.

Dream for him a savage vision:
A multitude of years will pass
20   When buildings in this upstart town
Again are lost in sea-drowned grass.
The forest will stay,
Nothing he loved gone down.

p.171 *Ian McDonald*

Notes and questions

Some of the poems in this section concern the death of a beloved relative, or the effect of such death on the persona; in others death is an occasion to discuss or reflect on life and experience; in still others death itself is discussed, complained about, or mocked. Since death is final and certain, but at the same time unknown, it exerts a powerful fascination on our minds and has always been a very popular theme in literature.

p.153 *It Was the Singing*

'long-metre' (line 4) – long-winded sermon.
Note how, by mentioning several people by name, the poet suggests a tight-knit community in mourning for one of its own; and how the daily problems as well as the sorrow are transcended through the singing at the funeral: 'It was then I know we people together' (lines 19–20).

p.154 *Grampa*

- We are told that the grandfather was very thin. This refers to his physical appearance; what are we told about his personality?

- What does the grandson foresee for his grandfather and for himself at the end of the poem?

p.155 *Long Distance*

'transport pass' (line 4) – pass to allow an elderly person to travel free on the buses.

- The father dealt with his grief and loss by pretending that his wife was still alive and might return at any moment. The son (the persona) believes that death is final; what is there in the final stanza that makes the son's position ironic?

p.155 *For Fergus*

Fergus Lawrence was a St Lucian intellectual and supporter of the arts who died quite young.

- The persona's attitude towards the dying Fergus is different from her attitude when he is dead. What is this difference, and can you explain it?

p.156 *Death the Leveller*

'sceptre' (line 5) – the ceremonial wand that symbolises the authority of a ruler.
'scythe' (line 8) – instrument used for reaping grain or for mowing grass or hay.
'victor-victim' (line 20) – death makes victims of all, including the 'victors'
in human conflicts.

- What is the point of the poet reminding us that all people are equally
  subject to death?
- What do the last two lines refer to?

p.157 *Death Came to See Me in Hot Pink Pants*

- Note that the personification of 'Death' in this poem accentuated by
  unusual attire makes it very dramatic. What do you think the poem is
  saying about death?
- How does the poet's awakening (line 20) resolve the questions raised by
  the poem, and what do the last two lines do to adjust our final
  perspective on this 'dream'?

p.158 *Dirge Without Music*

The persona knows what death means but does not accept it willingly – she
is protesting against death.

- Why is it that the 'elegant' (line 10) and 'fragrant' (line 11) flowers do
  not console the persona?
- The persona is aware that the protest is futile, so why does she make it?

p.158 *Death, be not proud . . .*

The argument in lines 5–6 is that rest and sleep are a little bit like death, and
since these give us some pleasure and renewal we should expect even more
from death.

In lines 9–12 the persona scoffs at the so-called 'pride' and 'power' of death
– death is no better than 'poison', 'war', 'sickness' and all the other agents
that kill men.

- The last two lines (13–14) indicate why the poet is not afraid of death.
  What is his confidence of survival based on?

p.159 *To an Athlete Dying Young*

- What do you think is meant by 'chaired' in line 2?
- Why is the town 'stiller' in line 8?

- According to the persona, why can it be considered better for the athlete to have died young?

p.160 ## Old Age Gets Up

- Compare this poem with 'Death Came to See Me in Hot Pink Pants'. Note that both make use of the device of personification and both involve references to apparel. What other techniques are used in this poem to make 'old age' more vivid and memorable?

p.160 ## Hot Summer Sunday

Compare this poem with 'Grampa' by Dennis Scott. Both grandparents appear still to be alive, although the grandchildren know that they are dead, and both inspire warm memories.

- What is the 'shallow trough' in which the grandfather is lying in line 15? What is it meant to echo from stanza 1?

- What is the point, in both poems, of comparing memories of the living grandfathers with their dead bodies?

p.161 ## Where Death was Kind

- In this poem death is depicted as a lover come to embrace the victim. For this reason the persona is at first jealous of death. Point out the lines where this feeling is made clear.

- Why is the image of death as lover particularly appropriate in this case?

p.162 ## Because I Could Not Stop for Death

'gossamer' (line 15) – a light transparent fabric.
'tippet' (line 16) – a kind of scarf or cape worn over or around the neck or shoulders.
'tulle' (line 16) – a fine net-like fabric used for veils, hats, etc.
Again, in this poem death is personified.
The 'swelling in the ground' (line 18) – refers to the grave in which the dead persona is buried.

- Note that Emily Dickinson in this poem faces the challenge of making the reader aware of what is going on, while keeping the persona only partly aware. This has the effect of a very powerful irony, reinforced by the matter-of-fact, conversational style.

p.163 *Brother Bone*

- Since death could not *actually* be his brother, what is the persona trying to say in this poem about his relationship to death? Perhaps this is summed up in the first three lines of the final stanza; but what does the last line mean?

p.164 *Ballad of Birmingham*

- Notice the form and the rhythm of this poem: four-line stanzas consisting of alternate four-stress and three-stress lines rhyming abcb. This is a very old and traditional rhythm and is called ballad metre. It was used in the traditional ballads that informed or reminded a community of important or troubling events in its history or recent past. These were usually sung to an audience. Later poets began to use the ballad form in order to benefit from the power, the mystery and the sense of occasion that had become attached to it.

- In this ballad notice how efficiently the story of the conflict between mother and child is rendered in the first four stanzas of dialogue; how the conflict appears to be happily resolved, only to give way to the shattering of all happiness in the mysterious explosion.

- Try writing the story in your own words.

p.165 *St Ann Saturday*

- Note that although the occasion being described is Miss Martha's funeral, the poem seems to celebrate life, rather than brood on death. What are some of the ways in which it does this?

- Why do you think the poet has another voice agree with the main speaker every now and then?

- What can you learn about the personality of the main speaker from what she says?

p.167 *Amerindian*

Title: 'Amerindian' – name of the native people in Guyana, where this poem is set.

- Why does the old Amerindian look awkward and out-of-place?

- What is the poet saying about the values of the 'town' and those of the native people of the interior?

Reading and enjoying poetry

Many students around CSEC age seem to be afraid of poems. They try to avoid them as much as possible, and when they can't, they approach them with dread, expecting the worst. It is true that for years the mean marks for the poetry questions on the CSEC paper have been among the lowest. This is a sad situation when one considers that poems exist mainly to give pleasure – as is the case with most creative writing. Poems are to be read aloud and enjoyed rather than approached as a difficult puzzle to be solved. Poems are in fact the most natural form of literary expression, the closest to ordinary speech and the first literary form that you encounter, long before you start going to school. The nursery rhymes, songs and jingles that you learned and enjoyed as very young children were poems – you could tell from looking at them. You can recognise a poem on the page because it consists of a string of individual lines, rather than paragraphs or solid blocks of writing. The lines can be long, marching or galloping right across the page, or short, descending swiftly down the middle like a narrow staircase. You can see how the very appearance of a poem can suggest movement or impart a feeling about it, even before the words are read. Whatever the appearance of poems on the page, however, they all share the same basic unit, the line, unlike prose where the unit is the sentence or the paragraph.

Because a poem is built of lines of words and is really meant to be read aloud, it has a special quality of sound which builds into a recognisable pattern that we call *rhythm*. All poems have rhythm, which consists of repeated patterns of stressed and unstressed syllables. Poems are like music, and in earlier times many were sung and accompanied by instruments such as the lute. So poems have a 'beat', like music, and the word rhythm is used to talk about both music and poetry. Note how the stressed (underlined) syllables determine the particular beat in the following stanza of Pratt's 'The Prize Cat':

And <u>when</u> I *mused* how <u>Time</u> had <u>thinned</u>
The <u>jun</u>gle *strains* with<u>in</u> the <u>cells</u>,
How <u>hu</u>man <u>hands</u> had <u>disci</u><u>plined</u>
Those <u>prow</u>ling <u>op</u>tic <u>par</u>al<u>lels</u> . . . (p. 7)

Here you get a regular pattern of an unstressed syllable followed by a stressed syllable. This is known as *iambic metre*. It is the most common metre in English poetry and is closest to the rhythm of ordinary speech in that language. There is no need for you to learn all the technical terms for the various metres at this stage, though you should be aware that there are several and they all produce different effects. What you need to notice as you read a poem aloud is the pace of the rhythm, whether quick or slow, and its appropriateness to the subject or *mood* of the poem. The rhythm can help you to understand a poem, as it is an important part of a poem's meaning. Always remember that in talking about a poem it is never any use simply to draw attention to the pattern of stresses nor to mention the technical terms for the various sound patterns; you must show that these have some relationship to the poem's meaning. If you can't relate a rhythmic effect that you notice to the poem's meaning, it is better not to say anything about it.

Another important sound device to be found in many poems is *rhyme*, when words at the ends of different lines have the same sound, as in:

Only the actions of the <u>just</u>
Smell sweet and blossom in their <u>dust</u>
(from Shirley's 'Death the Leveller', p. 156)

There is also *internal rhyme*, when a sound in the middle of a line is repeated at the end, but this should only be mentioned if it draws attention to something important or creates a special effect to emphasise some aspect of the poem's meaning. Sometimes rhymes occur in a regular pattern throughout the poem and the poem is said to have a *rhyme scheme*. In some poems the rhymes do not form a pattern and the poem is said to have *irregular rhyme*; in others the rhymes only occur in a few places, and this is called *occasional rhyme*. There are other sound devices you should know about, such as *assonance* and *alliteration* (see the Glossary of terms), and these all help to indicate the importance of sound to poetry. It is important to stress, therefore, the need to experience a poem's sound patterns by reading it aloud before attempting to write about it.

After you have noticed its physical appearance on the page and noted its sound patterns, you have to deal with the language of the poem – words and what they mean. We use the word *diction* to refer to the way words are used in a poem – not single words, usually, but the general quality of the words used. We speak of a poem's diction as being 'concrete' (where the words refer predominantly to real things), 'abstract' (where they refer mainly to ideas and imprecise feelings), 'colloquial' or 'formal', 'technical' or 'common', and so on. Another thing to remember about words in poems is that they don't only mean what the dictionary says they mean (*denote*). They also conjure up in your mind other words and associations, feelings and scraps of memory (particularly of other places and poems where you have encountered the same word in the past), ideas and experiences. This property of words in a poem is known as their ability to *connote* and the *connotative* meaning of a word is often more important in a poem than its *denotative* meaning. In this way poems, even very brief ones, expand ever outward and seem to become larger works with richer meanings and deeper feelings than appeared possible when you first saw them on the page.

Of course words are also woven into *images* and other *figures of speech*, which are very important in poetry. These paint pictures and appeal to all of our senses. Look at how the poet (Yeats, in this case) makes us see, hear and feel certain things in the following stanza from 'The Wild Swans at Coole':

> I have looked upon those brilliant creatures,
> And now my heart is sore.
> All's changed since I, hearing at twilight,
> The first time on this shore,
> The bell-beat of their wings above my head,
> Trod with a lighter tread.

As we read this stanza the *imagery* helps us to understand it by re-creating for us something of the experience of the feeling which prompted the poet to write the poem. Such communication of feeling and experience (and the pleasure to be had from it) is the main purpose of poetry. Types of image and specific figures of speech have names you should learn like *simile, metaphor, personification*, and so on (see the Glossary of terms).

Words, images and the other components of a poem work together to create the less concrete attributes that you also have to be aware of and discuss when you answer questions on poetry. For example, there is an overall feeling projected by a poem which in some cases builds powerfully to the point where it predominates and claims almost all our attention. This is called the *mood* or *atmosphere* of the poem. Some poems are written simply to create atmosphere or to evoke a particular mood, but in most poems it is possible to identify a mood or several moods as the poem progresses. For example, look at the mood created in the first six lines of Baugh's 'Sometimes in the Middle of the Story':

> Sometimes in the middle of the story something
> move outside the house, like
> it could be the wind, but is not the wind
> and the story-teller hesitate so slight
> you hardly notice it, and the children
> hold their breath and look at one another.

Here the poet has created a mood of hushed expectancy, almost foreboding, achieved mainly through the cumulative effect of the suggestiveness of words and the situation. Students sometimes confuse the mood of a poem with its *tone*. Tone is associated with the tone of voice, and therefore the attitude of the poet towards the subject of his poem. The tone can be 'detached', 'sympathetic', 'sarcastic', 'quarrelsome', and so on; whereas mood, as we have seen, is the predominant feeling created by the poem.

There are, of course, many types of poems. There are *narrative poems*, where the principal function is to tell a story and *descriptive poems*, which communicate ideas and feelings about people, objects and landscapes by describing selected details. There are *mood poems*, as described above, which also fall into the category called *lyrical poems*, which are usually written in the first person and express a state of mind or a process of thought or feeling. *Epic poems* are long narrative poems which are associated with the history or identity of a people. *Elegies*, or *elegiac poems* mourn the dead or look back with regret at something which no longer exists. There are also many terms for the various forms of poems (e.g. the sonnet form), but there is no need to learn all of these. Your teacher will tell you, as you study a particular poem, what category it belongs to; you can also check the notes on the poems at the end of each section.

These are some of the basic things you need to know about poems and how they communicate meaning. As with all things, detailed knowledge dispels fear! The more you read poetry and the more you practise trying to talk about it in the terms outlined here (and those taught in class), the less you will be afraid of poems. There is a world of enjoyment in a collection of poetry and your first attitude towards this one should be a desire to experience the pleasure of reading the poems – technical understanding will come afterwards. You can check on things you read about poetry by consulting the Glossary of terms.

Checklist for reading a poem

1 Subject matter
- Who is speaking? (speaker)
- In what situation? (occasion)
- To whom? (addressee)
- Privately or publicly?
- About what? (subject or theme)
- What is said? (thesis)
- Directly or indirectly?
- What common human concerns does this touch on? (universality)

2 Sound
- What does the sound pattern tell you?
- Is the rhythm quick or slow?
- Does the rhythm suit/reinforce the subject matter?
- Is there rhyme?
- Does the rhyme contribute to your understanding/enjoyment of the poem?
- Is there any interesting or appropriate use of alliteration/assonance?

3 Diction
- Are the words simple? Or complicated?
- Sophisticated? Or naive?
- Formal? Or conversational?
- Smooth? Or rough?
- Many-syllabled? Or monosyllabic?
- How does the diction contribute to meaning/mood?

4 Imagery
- Is the imagery striking? Or ordinary?
- Easily understood? Or obscure?
- Is the principal appeal to the sense of sight? Or hearing, touch, etc?
- Is the imagery functional? Or ornamental?
- Is the imagery symbolic?
- Is the symbolism natural? Conventional? Original?

5 Mood and tone
- How would you describe the mood of the poem?
- Is the poem more thoughtful than emotional?
- More emotional than thoughtful?
- Are thought and emotion balanced in the poem?
- Is the tone of the poem serious? Or light?
- Is it ironical? Satirical? Sentimental? Sincere? Flippant? etc.

6 Organic consistency
- Do all the items above fuse into an organic whole?
- Are there any elements (imagery, diction, etc.) which appear unsuited to the rest of the poem?
- Are there some elements which don't seem to have a good reason for being there?

7 Do you like the poem? If you were putting together an anthology of good poems, would you include the poem? For what particular reasons?

CSEC questions on poetry and how to answer them

Questions on the poems taken from this book will be part of Paper 2 of the CSEC English B Examination. The revised CSEC syllabus for this subject indicates that both poetry questions (of which students *must* answer one) will be so-called Type B questions, that is, questions of comparison of *two* texts. All poetry questions will therefore be comparative and will require that you know and have studied the *two* poems indicated. Here is a fairly straightforward example of this type of question taken from a past paper:

> Consider the poems 'During Wind and Rain' (Thomas Hardy) and 'Earth is Brown' (Shana Yardan).
>
> a   Show **two** ways in which the poems are about similar things and **one** way in which their subject matter differs.
> b   Select **two** images, **one** from **each** poem, that express similar ideas and show how they are similar.

As you can see from this question, you are expected to go into the exam with a fairly detailed knowledge of the texts of the poems; so it would be a good idea to memorise a significant number (at least) of the poems on the syllabus. Since there are never many more than twenty poems prescribed, this is not an impossible task.

Notice that the part (a) of the question above requires you to make a fairly simple comparison, though perhaps complicated by the specific **number** of tasks required: **two** points of similarity but **one** point of difference. Always remember too that it is never enough just to rattle off the points; if you can quote lines or phrases from the poems in answering you will score much more than the candidate whose imperfect knowledge of the poem confines him or her to an approximate paraphrase or a vague generalisation. This part of the question tests mainly knowledge and the ability to compare. In part (b) you are required to focus upon poetic language and the poet's technique – you must know what an image is, should identify it specifically (simile, metaphor, etc.), choose appropriate examples and discuss or explain what idea is expressed through them and how.

Here is a different example of the same type of question, taken from a past paper:

Consider the poems 'Journey of the Magi' (Eliot) and 'The Shaddhu of Couva' (Walcott).

a   How are the situations in these poems similar?
b   Compare the moods of the speakers in the two poems.
c   With close reference to the poems, show how **each** uses landscape and physical detail to achieve its effect.

The first part of the question is again concerned with the basic skill of *comparison*. In part (b) you are asked to assess and compare the 'moods' of the speakers – a more difficult concept, requiring a higher-level skill; it is this part of the question that will test knowledge specific to the genre of poetry, and that will separate the grade one candidates from the others. Most of you will be able to mention a few details of physical landscape in response to part (c), but only the better among you will be able to quote the relevant lines accurately and to explain the relationship between each *detail* and the *effect* created in the poem.

Your teacher will probably try to devise similar questions using the poems in this book. Perhaps these will start with poems that are obviously similar, like the two poems about thunderstorms in the 'Nature' section: 'Rain Storm' by Sasenarine Persaud (p.8) and 'An African Thunderstorm' by David Rubadiri (p.9). The question your teacher gives you might be something like the following:

Consider the poems 'Rain Storm' (Persaud) and 'An African Thunderstorm' (Rubadiri).

a   Compare the language used in the descriptions of the storms.
b   With specific references, point out **one** difference in the way the humans present in the poems respond to the storm.
c   Select an important image from each poem and show how it contributes to the effect of the poem.

Here you have your basic comparison in the first part, but you are being asked to compare not content, but language. Part (b) draws your attention specifically to content and requires good knowledge of the texts. Part (c) requires the higher-level skills involved in the discussion of specific techniques and their effects.

Model answers

Model answers are useful both to teachers and students, but as they are supposed to be perfect, it would be more realistic to look at answers at different levels of competence, so that you may judge the quality. Consider the following answer to the question we concocted in the previous section on the two poems about thunderstorms:

(a) The language in 'Rain Storm' deals mostly with the rain water. The poet talks about 'waterangels', 'jets/Of silver water' and 'spinning droplets'. This kind of language make the storm seem real, as though the reader is in the middle of it. On the other hand, however, 'An African Thunderstorm' talks first about the clouds gathering for the storm. These are described as 'pregnant' and like 'a cloud of locusts'. The wind is also 'whistling', but we don't really see any rain as in the first poem. In this poem the effect of the language is to have us in suspense, like the excited children waiting for the storm to come.

(b) It seems as if the only human present in 'Rain Storm' is the poet himself, and he reacts by thinking of God and of melting into God and the rain. In the other poem, though, there are many people, such as the children and the mothers waiting for the storm. These seem to be happy that the storm is coming – the poet talks of 'delighted children' and babies and mothers 'darting about'. So this is one difference between the two poems: in one the human present reacts religiously but in the other people are happy and having fun.

(c) The image I select from 'Rain Storm' is 'This rage of waterangels/On zinc'. This is very effective since in that part of the world the houses are probably covered with zinc sheets so we can see the water running off in our minds. In 'An African Thunderstorm' a good image is the simile where the poet says the clouds are 'Like a madman chasing nothing'. This is truly effective because madmen do chase around after nothing and the clouds are behaving likewise. Both are effective poems about storms, though different.

This is the kind of answer often given on CSEC scripts. The candidate is not insensitive to the poems; he/she gets close to the gist of what is required in part (a) but the answer gets progressively worse as an attempt is made to deal with the more demanding sections of the question. In (b) he/she sees what the question asks for but cannot express it well enough and in (c) the choice of images is poor and he/she just cannot discuss their effect. Poor language skills tend to shipwreck this answer.

Here is a different answer to the same question. This student chooses the same things to talk about in some cases, but does it with greater sensitivity and skill – and not only remembers the poems, but is able to discuss them as literature. Notice that the second answer is written as a continuous essay, *following the instructions on the CSEC paper*, so will not be penalised for poor organisation of response. The second candidate also has a much better command of language. While the first candidate might have ended up with half marks for the question, the second should score close to full marks:

There is some similarity in the language used to describe the storms in the two poems. Both poets are anxious to convey the power of the storms and the awesome forces of nature. In 'Rain Storm' the words used suggest energy and movement: the gutter 'spews' jets of water and the droplets of water are 'spinning'. There is violence in the 'rage of waterangels' and the 'slap of thunder'. For most of 'An African Thunderstorm' the storm is brewing, rather than actually raging, but the language is similarly heightened and we are told of the wind 'whistling' by the trees that 'bend to let it pass'. Towards the end, as the storm breaks, we are told of the 'jagged, blinding flashes of the lightning' and 'the smell of fire and smoke'.

Despite these similarities, however, the language used creates quite different moods in the two poems. In 'Rain Storm' the image of the clouds touching the river suggests the joining of heaven and earth, and the human presence in the poem, the persona, is moved to think of God. The mood is quite solemn and the persona seems to be having a religious experience, especially towards the end of the poem when he and the rain and God all melt into each other – no doubt part of the effect of the ceaselessly running water which seems to liquify the world.

In 'An African Thunderstorm', despite the awesome power of the elements, the mood among the people is one of happy expectancy; this is especially true of the children. The humans in this poem are not standing in quiet contemplation of the storm as seems to be the case in 'Rain Storm'; rather the children are screaming with excitement and the women are darting about, presumably making sure that clothes and grain, etc. are placed under shelter. In the final stanza the storm winds rip off the people's clothes in an appropriate gesture of ecstatic enjoyment.

In 'Rain Storm' also there is an image of clothing, as the poet describes the river reacting to the storm by 'baring her frothy/Underwear at thunder touch'. This is a very arresting image and it seems particularly appropriate when we consider that the wind and water do churn the river to foam. But there is also the word 'touch', which suggests something sensual, particularly when associated with 'underwear'. This is not necessarily out of keeping with the religious imagery as it does express the ecstasy of the melting together of all things.

My favourite image in 'An African Thunderstorm' is that of the storm clouds 'Gathering to perch on hills/Like dark sinister wings'; this captures perfectly the brooding presence of the storm before it actually bursts. The descriptive accuracy of the image is matched by the thrill of the unknown contained in the word 'sinister'. The violent arrival of the storm in the last stanza is the fulfilment of this image. Both are fine poems but I identify more with the community in 'An African Thunderstorm' than with the awe-struck persona of 'Rain Storm'.

Very few students at CSEC level will be able to write as good an answer as this one. Nevertheless it, or something like it, should be the aim of better candidates. Most of you should be satisfied to achieve something in between the two responses given – better than the first and attempting to approach the second. This should be the aim of you and your teachers.

Glossary of terms

alliteration a sound effect caused by the repetition of stressed consonant sounds, as in the line: 'While she was *y*et too *y*oung to crawl' ('Ana', p. 25).

assonance sound effect consisting of the repetition of stressed vowel sounds, as in the lines 'like the closing of some aweful book/a too-long story' ('For Rosa Parks' p. 111).

blank verse unrhymed five-stress lines, principally of iambic metre (iambic pentameters). Milton's *Paradise Lost* and most of Shakespeare's plays are written in blank verse.

caesura a pause in a line of poetry, usually dependent on the sense of the line and indicated by a strong punctuation mark.

connotation the secondary meanings and associations suggested to the reader by a particular word or phrase, as opposed to denotation, or dictionary meaning.

couplet two lines of the same metre which rhyme.

denotation the meaning of a word according to the dictionary, as opposed to its connotations.

elegy a formal poem lamenting the death of a particular person.

epic a long narrative poem, usually celebrating some aspect of the history or identity of a people. Dante's *Divine Comedy* and Milton's *Paradise Lost* are examples of epic poems.

epic simile a simile extending over several lines, in which the object of comparison is described at great length.

eye rhyme a pair of syllables which appear to the eye as though they should rhyme, but which do not, like 'have' and 'wave'.

figurative language non-literal expressions used to convey more vividly certain ideas and feelings; includes such figures as simile, metaphor and personification.

form either the appearance of poetry on the page or a way of referring to the structure of the poem – its division into stanzas, etc.

free verse poetry that has no regular rhythmic pattern (metre).

hyperbole a kind of figurative language consisting of exaggeration or overstatement.

imagery vivid description of an object or a scene; the term is also applied to figurative language, particularly to examples of simile and metaphor.

irony   a device whereby the apparent meaning of a phrase or passage is different from the meaning it is really intended to convey.

lyric   a type of poetry that is a personal statement evoking a mood or expressing a certain feeling.

metaphor   a type of figurative language in which one thing is described in a way that identifies it with something else, for example when the poet likens the heartbeat to a frightened mare in these lines from 'Coming Out' (page 29).

> A frightened mare
> galloping down cobbled
> streets on a stormy night;
> your heartbeat fills the room.

metre   the regular pattern of stressed and unstressed syllables that we hear over several lines of poetry.

mood   the dominant feeling evoked by the words, images and other devices used in a poem.

onomatopoeia   a word or group of words whose sound suggests its meaning, like 'hiss' or 'murmur'.

pastoral   a highly conventional poetic form which celebrates the world of shepherds and other country people.

personification   when the poet refers to an inanimate object or an abstract quality as though it were a living person, as in John Donne's lines, 'Death, be not proud, though some have called thee/Mighty and dreadful' (p. 158).

quatrain   a four-line stanza or group of lines, usually rhyming.

rhyme   the repetition of the last stressed vowel sound in a word together with any unstressed sounds that follow, as in gate, late, and cover, lover. There are special terms that describe different kinds of rhyme (see notes on rhyme in the section Reading and enjoying poetry).

rhyme scheme   the pattern of rhymed endings of lines within a stanza or short poem. The first rhymed sounds can be labelled a, the second b and so on, so that the rhyme scheme in E. J. Pratt's 'The Prize Cat' (p. 7) is abab, cdcd, etc.

rhythm   the recurrence of groups of stressed and unstressed syllables in lines of poetry. (See notes on rhyme in the section Reading and enjoying poetry.)

run-on lines   lines in which the meaning leads you to run swiftly beyond the end of the line and into the next line to complete the syntax and the sense, as in the lines:

> . . . you think I wouldn't rather
> take my blood seasoned in fat
> black pudding, like everyone else? ('Ol' Higue', p. 128)

simile   a figure of speech in which an explicit comparison is made between two things, using 'like', 'as' or 'than', as in '. . . the sun toils like a fisherman/with a hard tide to beat' ('The Tourists', p. 107).

sonnet   a form of poem almost always consisting of fourteen five-stressed lines. The two main types of sonnet are the English or Shakespearean sonnet (distinguished by its final couplet), and the Italian or Petrarchan sonnet, consisting of a group of eight lines (the *octave*) followed by a group of six lines (the *sestet*).

stanza   a group of lines forming one of the divisions of a poem.

stress   refers to the prominence or emphasis given to certain words or syllables when they are spoken. Stress is a prominent feature of English speech and therefore of the rhythm of poetry in English.

synedoche   a figure of speech in which a part is used for a whole, an individual for a class, or the reverse of these. For example, $5 per head means $5 per person.

tercet   a three-line stanza or a group of three lines within a stanza or a poem.

tone   the poet's attitude or tone of voice. The tone gives a clue as to how the poem is to be read, or reinforces other aspects of the poem's meaning. (See the note on mood and tone in the section Reading and enjoying poetry.)

Index

Acknowledgements

Every effort has been made to contact copyright holders of material reproduced in this book. Any omissions will be rectified in subsequent printings if notice is given to the publishers.

'A View of the Caribbean and Its Memories of Our Not-So-Recent Collective Past' by Funso Aiyejina. © Funso Aiyejina. Reprinted with the kind permission of the author. 'Man With A Hook' by Margaret Atwood, from THE CIRCLE GAME published by House of Anassi Press in 1966. Copyright © 1966 Margaret Atwood. Reprinted with permission of Curtis Brown Ltd, London. 'Sonnets from China XV' and 'Lullaby' by W H Auden, from COLLECTED POEMS, published by Faber and faber Limited. Reprinted with permission of the publishers. 'It Was the Singing' and 'Responsibility' by Edward Baugh which first appeared in IT WAS THE SINGING published by Sandberry Press in 2000 © Edward Baugh 2000, and 'The Carpenter's Complaint' which first appeared in A TALE FROM THE RAINFOREST published by Sandberry Press in 1988. © Edward Baugh 1998, are used by permission of the poet Edward Baugh, and Sandberry Press. 'Dreaming Black Boy' by James Berry from WHEN I DANCE copyright © James Berry 1988, and 'Early Innocence' by James Berry, from FRACTURED CIRCLES, New Beacon Books. © James Berry 1979. Reprinted by permission of PFD (www.pfd.co.uk) on behalf of James Berry. 'El Greco: Espolio' by Earle Birney, reprinted by permission of The Honourable Madam Justice Wailan Low, as Literary Executor for the Estate of Earle Birney. 'Naima' by Kamau Braithwaite. Copyright © Kamau Braithwaite. 'South', 'Part 1 of Ancestors' and 'The Emigrants' – extract from, from THE ARRIVANTS published by OUP 1973. Reprinted with permission of the publishers. 'A Song in the Front Yard' by Gwendolyn Brooks. © Gwendolyn Brooks. Reprinted by Consent of Brooks Permissions. 'West Indies USA' and 'Coming Out' by Stuart Brown, from LUGARDS' BRIDGE published by Seren Books 1989. © 1989 Stuart Brown, and 'Test Match Sabina Park' from ZINDER published by Poetry Wales Press 1986 © 1986 Stuart Brown. Reprinted with the kind permission of the author. 'Drought' and 'The Tourists' by Wayne Brown from ON THE COAST published by Andre Deutsch, London 1973. © Wayne Brown 1973. Reprinted with the kind permission of the author. 'It is the Constant Image of Your Face' by Dennis Brutus. From A SIMPLE LUST published by Heinemann Oxford. 'Childhood of Voice' by Martin Carter, from SELECTED POEMS published by Peepal Tree Books. Reprinted by permission of the publishers. 'This is the dark time, my love' by Martin Carter. 'Cold As Heaven' by Judith Ortiz Cofer, from REACHING FOR THE MAINLAND published by Bilingual Review Press. © Judith Ortiz Cofer. Reprinted with permission of Bilingual Review Press. 'Forgive My Guilt' by Robert P Tristram Coffin. Reprinted with the kind permission of the Estate of Robert P. Tristram Coffin. 'Counter' by Merle Collins, from LADY IN A BOAT published by Peepal Tree Books. Reprinted by permission of the publishers. 'Edwin Arlington Robinson' by Richard Cory, from THE CHILDREN OF THE NIGHT first published in 1897. 'St. Ann Saturday' and 'Elsa's Version' by Christine Craig. © Christine Craig. 'Coolie Son' and

'Coolie Mother' by David Dabydeen, from COOLIE ODYSSEY, 1990 © 1990 David Dabydeen. Reprinted with permission of Anthony Harwood Ltd on behalf of the author. 'Mama Dot's Treatise' by Fred D'Aguiar, from MAMA DOT published by Chatto & Windus. Reprinted by permission of The Random House Group Ltd. 'Oars' by Mahadai Das, from BONES published by Peepal Tree Books. Reprinted by permission of the publishers. 'Return' (for Kamau Braithwaite) by Kwame Dawes, from NEW AND SELECTED POEMS published by Peepal Tree Books. Reprinted by permission of the publishers. 'Hate' by David Eva, from SUNBURST edited by Ian Gordon published by Heinemann. 'Ultimate' by Howard Fergus © Howard Fergus. 'The Sound of Trees' by Robert Frost, from THE POETRY OF ROBERT FROST edited by Edward Connery Lathem, published by Jonathan Cape. Reprinted by permission of The Random House Group Ltd. 'Geography Lesson' by Zulfikar Ghose, from JETS FROM ORANGE published by Macmillan London Copyright © 1967 by Zulfikar Ghose. Reprinted by permission of Sheil Land Associates Ltd on behalf of the author. 'The Woman Speaks to the Man Who has Employed her Son', 'The Sleeping Zemis', 'For Rosa Parks', 'My Mother's Sea Chanty' and 'For My Mother (May I Inherit Half Her strength' by Lorna Goodison, from GUINEA WOMAN published by Carcanet Press Limited, reprinted with permission of the publishers. 'Schooldays' and 'Caribbean History' by Stanley Greaves, from HORIZONS published by Peepal Tree Books. Reprinted by permission of the publishers. 'Limbo-Man' by Judith Hamilton, from RAIN CARVERS published by Sandberry Press in 1992. © Judith Hamilton. Reprinted with the kind permission of the author. 'Listening to Sirens' and extract from 'Long Distance 11' by Tony Harrison. © Tony Harrison. Reprinted by permission of Gordon Dickerson on behalf of Tony Harrison. 'Those Winter Sundays' by Robert Hayden, from ANGLE OF ASCENT: NEW AND COLLECTED POEMS. Copyright © 1966 by Robert Hayden. Used by permission of Liveright Publishing Corporation. 'Mid-Term Break' by Seamus Heaney, from DEATH OF A NATURALIST published by Faber and faber Limited. Reprinted by permission of the publishers. 'Hot Summer Sunday' by A L Hendriks. 'Liminal' by Kendel Hippolyte, from BIRTHRIGHT published by Peepal Tree Books. Reprinted by permission of the publishers. 'I Will Lift Up Mine Eyes', 'Visions of Us' and 'Brother Bone' by Kendel Hippolyte. Copyright © Kendel Hippolyte. Reprinted with the kind permission of the author. 'Girl Reporter' by Philip Hobsbaum, from THE PLACE'S FAULT AND OTHER POEMS published by Macmillan in 1964. Reprinted with the kind permission of the author. 'The Lady's Maid's Song' by John Hollander, from SELECTED POETRY . Copyright © 1993 John Hollander. Used by permission of Alfred A. Knopf, a division of Random House Inc. 'Himself at Last' by Slade Hopkinson, from SNOWSCAPE WITH SIGNATURE published by Peepal Tree Books. Reprinted by permission of the publishers. 'Theme for English B' by Langston Hughes, from THE COLLECTED POEMS OF LANGSTON HUGHES published by Alfred A. Knopf Inc. Reprinted by permission of David Higham Associates Ltd. 'Bayonet Charge' by Ted Hughes, from THE HAWK IN THE RAIN published by Faber and Faber, and 'Old Age Gets Up' from MOORTOWN reprinted by permission of the publishers. 'For Fergus' by Jane King, which first appeared in FELLOW TRAVELLER published by Sandberry Press, 1994. © Jane King 1994, used by permission of the poet, Jane King and Sandberry Press. 'Sad Steps' by Philip Larkin, from COLLECTED POEMS published by Faber and Faber Limited. Reprinted by permission of the publishers. 'Corruption' by Freddy Macha, from NEW POETRY FROM AFRICA edited by Jack

Mapanje from Malawi, published by Heinemann in the 1983 Summer Fires Collection. © Freddy Macha. Reprinted with the kind permission of the author. 'Ars Poetica' by Archibald MacLeish, from COLLECTED POEMS 1917-1982. Copyright © 1985 by the Estate of Archibald MacLeish. Reprinted by permission of Houghton Mifflin Company. All rights reserved. 'Light Love' by Roger Mais, © Roger Mais. 'The Listeners' by Walter De La Mare, from THE COMPLETE POEMS OF WALTER DE LA MARE 1969 (USA 1970). Reprinted by permission of The Literary Trustees of Walter de la Mare and the Society of Authors as their representatives. 'Where Death Was Kind' by Una Marson. 'Orchids', 'Silk Cotton Trees' and 'Parasite' by Hazel Simmons-McDonald. © Copyright Hazel Simmons-McDonald. Reprinted with the kind permission of the author. 'God's Work' and 'Amerindian' by Ian McDonald, from MERCY WARD published by Peterloo Poets, 1988. Reprinted with the permission of the publishers. 'The Lynching' by Claude McKay, from HARLEM SHADOWS. Reprinted Courtesy of the Literary Representative for the Works of Claude McKay, Schomburg Center for Research in Black Culture, The New York Public Library, Astor, Lenox and Tilden Foundations. 'Ana', 'Gull' , 'River Girl' , 'Koriabo' and 'Ol' Higue' by Mark McWatt. © Mark McWatt. Reprinted with the kind permission of the author. 'Dirge Without Music' by Edna St. Vincent Millay, from SELECTED POEMS published by Carcanet Press Ltd. Reprinted with permission of the publishers. 'A Stone's Throw' by Elma Mitchell, from PEOPLE ETCETERA: POEMS NEW AND SELECTED, published by Peterloo Poets. Reprinted with permission of the publishers. 'Jesus is Nailed to the Cross' by Pamela Mordecai, from DE MAN published by Sister Vision Press. © Pamela Mordecai. 'Examination Centre' and 'Departure Lounge' by Mervyn Morris from EXAMINATION CENTRE, first published by New Beacon Books in 1992, 'Little Boy Crying' by Mervyn Morris, from THE POND first published by New Beacon Books in 1973, and 'The Daemon-Brother' by Mervyn Morris from SHADOWBOXING first published by New Beacon Books in 1979. Reprinted by permission of the publishers. 'Why I'm Not A Painter' by Frank O'Hara from WHY I'M NOT A PAINTER published by Carcanet Press Ltd, reprinted with permission of the publishers. 'Once Upon A Time' by Gabriel Okara. 'Ethics' by Linda Pastan from WAITING FOR MY LIFE by Linda Pastan. Copyright © 1981 Linda Pastan. Used by permission of W W Norton & Company Inc. 'Rain Storm' by Sesenarine Persaud. © Sesenarine Persaud. Reprinted with the kind permission of the author. 'Stillborn', 'Mirror' and 'Pheasant' by Sylvia Plath from COLLECTED POEMS published by Faber and Faber Limited. Reprinted by permission of the publishers. 'Appartment Neighbours' by Velma Pollard, from SHAME TREES DON'T GROW HERE published by Peepal Tree Books. Reprinted by permission of the publishers. 'Sea Wall' by Velma Pollard © Velma Pollard. Reprinted with the kind permission of the author. 'The Prize Cat' by E. J. Pratt, from COLLECTED POEMS published by The University of Toronto Press. Reprinted with permission of the publishers. 'Ballad of Birmingham' by Dudley Randall. Reprinted with the kind permission of Melba J Boyd. 'Janet Waking' by John Crowe Ransom, from SELECTED POEMS published by Carcanet Press Ltd. Reprinted by permission of the publishers. 'I Knew A Woman' and 'My Papa's Waltz' by Theodore Roethke, from COLLECTED POEMS published by Faber and Faber Limited, Reprinted by permission of the publishers. 'The Teacher' by Thomas Romano, from ENGLISH JOURNAL March 1982 © National Council of Teachers of English. Reprinted with permission of the publishers. 'Death Came To See Me In Hot Pink Pants' by Heather Royes, from

DAYS AND NIGHTS OF THE BLUE IGUANA published by Peepal Tree Books. Reprinted by permission of the publishers. 'An African Thunderstorm' from AN AFRICAN THUNDERSTORM AND OTHER POEMS by David Rubadiri, published by EAEP, reprinted with permission of the publishers. 'Silver Wedding' by Vernon Scannell. © Vernon Scannell. Reprinted with the kind permission of the author. 'Epitaph', 'Grampa' and 'Infidelities' by Dennis Scott, from UNCLE TIME. Copyright © 1973 by Dennis Scott. Reprinted by permission of the University of Pittsburgh Press. 'A Comfort of Crows' by Dennis Scott. © Dennis Scott. 'Birdshooting Season' by Olive Senior, from TALKING OF TREES, 'Childhood' and 'Colonial Girls School' by Olive Senior. © Olive Senior. Reprinted by permission of Olive Senior and the Watkins/Loomis Agency. 'My Parents' by Stephen Spender from COLLECTED POEMS 1928-1985. Reprinted by permission of the publishers. 'Travelling Through The Dark' by William Stafford. Copyright © 1962, 1998 by the Estate of William Stafford. Reprinted from THE WAY IT IS: NEW AND SELECTED POEMS with the permission of Graywolf Press, Saint Paul, Minnesota. 'In the New World' by Elaine Terranova, first published in THE CULT OF THE RIGHT HAND published by Doubleday 1991. © Elaine Terranova 1991. Reprinted with the kind permission of the author. 'Green Beret' by Ho Thien, from SUNBURST edited by Ian Gordon published by Heinemann. 'The Moor' by R S Thomas, from SELECTED POEMS: 1946-1968 (Bloodaxe Books 1986) Reprinted with permission of Bloodaxe Books. 'A View of Dingle Bay, Ireland' by Ralph Thompson from MOVING ON published by Peepal Tree Books. Reprinted by permission of the publishers. 'Ahmad' by Edwin Thumboo. © Edwin Thumboo. Reprinted with the kind permission of the author. 'Swimming Chenango Lake' by Charles Tomlinson. © Charles Tomlinson. Reprinted with the kind permission of the author. 'Revelation' by H A Vaughan, from SANDY LAND AND OTHER POEMS 2ND Edition 1985 published by The Book Place. 'Landscape Painter, Jamaica' by Vivian Virtue, from WINGS OF THE EVENING: SELECTED POEMS OF VIVIAN VIRTUE published by Ian Randle Publishers, Kingston, Jamaica, edited by A L McLeod. 'A Lesson for this Sunday', 'La belle qui fut'/Tales of the Islands', 'La Loupgarou/ Tales of the Islands' and 'A Letter from Brooklyn' by Derek Walcott, from COLLECTED POEMS 1948-1984, and 'Saint Lucia's First Communion' by Derek Walcott from THE ARKANSAS TESTAMENT published by Faber and Faber Limited. reprinted by permission of the publishers. 'Journal for Melanie' by David Williams. © David Williams. Reprinted with the kind permission of the author. 'Photos' by Cynthia Wilson, from THE HIBISCUS BEARS A BLUE FLOWER self published by Cynthia Wilson in 2004 © Cynthia Wilson 2004. Reprinted with the kind permission of the author